China on the Edge

Chinese Border Provinces and Chinese Security Policy

Attention Authors

'We Convert Fighters into Writers'. That's the motto of Manas Publications since more than four decades. Our message to the world is that India can win the battle not only by the bullet but also by the pen. There is no dearth of intellectuals in our country, but their knowledge is confined to them only. No sincere effort has been made by any other publisher to channelise their knowledge in national interest. That is why the talent of a large number of intellectuals remains latent. An author transforms his knowledge into a manuscript, and it is our job to spread his/her knowledge by converting it into a beautiful book. For over four decades, Manas has been motivating the intellectuals by publishing their manuscripts and would like to publish your manuscript too. If you or your colleagues have any manuscript ready for publication or are working on it, kindly contact us with detailed synopsis and list of contents. We will transform your work into a valuable publication. If you wish, we can also suggest you the suitable subjects for writing the books related to your area of expertise. Manas is known for its publishing quality and commitments. We take utmost care in production and give wide publicity to the book as well as its author through our national and international distribution network.

China
on the
Edge

Chinese Border Provinces and Chinese Security Policy

Carla Freeman
Drew Thompson

Manas Publications
(We Convert Fighters into Writers)
New Delhi-110002 (INDIA)

Manas Publications
(We Convert Fighters into Writers)
(Publishers, Library Suppliers, Importers & Exporters)
4402/5-A, Ansari Road (Opp. HDFC Bank)
Darya Ganj, New Delhi-110 002 (India)
Off. 011-23260783, 23265523, Res. 011-23842660
Fax: 011-23272766
E-mail: manaspublications@gmail.com
manaspublications@yahoo.com
Website:www. manaspublications.in

Carla Freeman
Drew Thompson

2014

ISBN: 978-81-7049-483-6
₹ 595/-

Printed in India at
H.S. Offsets, Delhi
and published by Mrs Suman Lata for
Manas Publications, 4402/5-A,
Ansari Road, (Opp HDFC Bank),
Darya Ganj, New Delhi-110 002 (INDIA)

Contents

Foreword

China on the Edge: Cooperation or Control

As violence rocked Tibet in 2008 followed by Xinjiang in 2009, China delivered an apparently contradictory message to the international community. Its spokespersons asserted that events in these regions were "strictly an internal affair;" in the same breath, they sharply condemned "external forces" for inciting the violence. What might appear to be a contradiction distills the intense anxieties that underlie China's perception of the heavily minority regions that lie along its land borders with other states and Beijing's acute awareness that in these regions international and domestic security are closely intertwined.[1]

China's ascent to a position of international wealth and power is being felt nowhere more immediately than

1. Drew Thompson is the Director of China Studies and Starr Senior Fellow at the Center for the National Interest. Carla Freeman is an Associate Research Professor in the China Studies department at Johns Hopkins University's School of Advanced International Studies.

along its borders. A crumbling Qing empire followed by a Chinese state struggling first against external attack and then domestic instability left many of China's international boundaries unsettled, heavily populated by non-Han minorities, with areas along the outer extent of its territorial control that were both poverty stricken and in many respects weakly governed. China's resurgence has brought with it a political and economic push to its sovereign edge, where it has sought to complete the process of nation building to the outer limits of its territorial sovereignty and extend its trade-oriented model for economic growth.

With this push to the edge, China's influence in the countries across its territorial borders is growing. Apart from major military powers, Russia and India, which have long loomed large along China's borders and high on China's list of security concerns, most of the 14 states that share China's more than 22,000 kilometer land boundary are comparatively small in stature. These are states that, if they existed in more or less their current form before the early 1990s, have historically depended on relationships with external powers to preserve their independence. Most are former Soviet clients (Pakistan excepted), and some, North Korea and to some extent Vietnam, effectively exploited both Chinese and Soviet influence during their recent history. Looking across China's relationships with these lesser states—from economically struggling Laos, to militarily and economically formidable Vietnam—their growing ties to China are clear. China's deepening relationships with its neighbors include trade flows in which China has become a top trade partner; energy relationships where China is both top customer and supplier; military cooperation; to infrastructure development, including road and dam construction; and new currency swap arrangements in which transactions are conducted directly without involving the US dollar in otherwise internationally nonconvertible Chinese currency.

These developments mark an expansion of Chinese influence in its frontiers or the areas along its international borders not seen since Mao Zedong reunified China and reestablished Chinese control over a large portion of Qing imperial territory. The potential for tensions between China and Russia over China's growing role in Russia's traditional Central Asian sphere is well studied. China's growing presence in the lesser countries along its borders, however, is extending China's influence into areas now also identified with American interests. Certainly, China has shown cooperation, even leadership, in international efforts to mitigate regional security crises involving some of these states, playing a leading role in the Six Party process most notably. It is uncertain, however, if China's objectives go beyond reducing the potential for serious disruptions to the status quo where these states are concerned or extend to the ability to exercise more decisive influence over the direction of policies in these countries, with implications for US policy. The recent financial crisis and the shift in military focus by the US to neighboring Afghanistan, as well as intensifying concerns about energy security to fuel China's economic expansion and growing oil and gas consumption amid volatile energy prices are among the factors reshaping the environment in which China is formulating policy toward its periphery. As Chinese confidence in economic globalization and in its ability to negotiate through dialogue with the U.S. the strategic space it needs to serve its increasingly global interests appears to be waning, its growing influence within the countries along its borders has the potential result in policies inimical to the objectives and initiatives of the US and its allies. Some might argue that this is already an emerging pattern in China's more assertive posture on maritime borders in the South and East China Seas.[2]

---

2. Carla Freeman, "China's Strategic Shift: What Reassurance?" Draft in peer review: (2011).

Not well understood is how China views its own frontier regions in this context and the role they play both in China's thinking about its security policy and in the formulation of Chinese security policy, including toward its neighboring states. As the following chapters will show, China's land borders are the objects of insecurity on the part of Beijing for a tangle of reasons. China's border areas include concentrations of ethnic minority populations that continue to represent hot zones for potentially contagious minority unrest within China. They are also seen as particularly vulnerable to the impact of external forces beyond China's control, making them places where Beijing's concerns about China's domestic stability and international vulnerabilities may converge. These land borders are after all staggeringly long. They extend for tens of thousands of kilometers, much of their length difficult-to-monitor terrain, from the oxygen-deprived heights of the Himalayas to the hills and valleys of its borders with Myanmar, Laos, and Vietnam. Six of China's neighboring states were found in the "alert" category of the Fund for Peace and Foreign Policy's 2009 Failed States Index.[3] The minority groups along China's largely porous land borders also represent potentially fertile ground for transborder ethno-nationalism, fueled perhaps, as in the case of Tibet in China's view, by groups beyond China's borders with irredentist claims on Chinese territory. Border regions are by their nature zones of unpredictability, places at the limits of states direct control, where international relationships get intimate and tensions can have significant international consequences.

After 2002, China's Central Committee called the "good neighbor" principle among China foreign policy priorities,

---

3. These states are Afghanistan, Myanmar, Nepal, North Korea, Pakistan, and Tajikistan.

second only to maintaining great power relations.[4] China stepped up efforts to cultivate, in Chinese Premier Wen Jiabao's words "amicable, peaceful and prosperous neighbors" ("mulin, anlin, fulin"), through border stabilization and ways to promote confidence-building and mutual trust.[5] This contributed to the conclusion of a long list of boundary agreements between China and its neighbors that year alone.[6] The resulting progress toward resolving most of its border demarcation issues with its neighbors eliminated a key source of tension between it and many territorially contiguous states and opened the door to closer bilateral and multilateral relations.

But closer relationships are also more complicated and

---

4. In 1993, Li Peng alluded to the importance of beneficial and friendly relations with neighboring states as a significant dimension of Chinese foreign policy. It was in the political report of the 16th Party Congress (2002), that a policy of "good neighbors and partners with neighboring countries" (yulin weishan, yilin weiban,) appeared for first time, see Shulan Ye, "China's Regional Policy in East Asia and its Characteristics," China Policy Institute School of Contemporary Chinese Studies, The University of Nottingham, Discussion Paper 66, (October 2010): 5, available at http://www.nottingham.ac.uk/cpi/documents/discussion-papers/discussion-paper-66-china-regional-policy-shulan-ye.pdf.
5. Wen Jiabao in 2003, see Chien-pung Chung, The "Good Neighbour Policy" in the Context of China's Foreign Relations," China: An International Journal, Volume 7, Number 1, (March 2009): 116.
6 "China's Territorial and Boundary Affairs," Ministry of Foreign Affairs, June 30, 2003: (http://www.mfa.gov.cn/eng/wjb/zzjg/tyfls/tyfl/2626/t22820.htm.) 3. These states are Afghanistan, Myanmar, Nepal, North Korea, Pakistan, and Tajikistan.

as China's interests towards its neighbors have grown, so have the challenges of managing its relationships with them. Porous borders to foster cross-border trade creates an enabling environment for cross-border pathologies, from illicit trade to disease to organized crime and even terrorism, all of which test the capacity of state regulation and control, and represent challenges to economic growth. Closer relations between neighboring states also hold the potential to constrain the flexibility and freedom of action in foreign policy by the states, given the ability of the states to affect conditions across their mutual borders.

China's border concerns thus extend beyond the well known hot spots of Xinjiang and Tibet to varying degrees elsewhere along China's land borders as well. Absent the high profile international issues that intersect with local tensions as they have done in Tibet and Xinjiang, these regions may not make front-page news in the western press. But each presents its own challenges for the Chinese state in terms of concerns about domestic stability and development, and as places bordering diverse and often politically unstable international neighbors. The relationships we examine provide a picture of the range of challenges China faces and how it manages this complex dimension of its security policy.

This requires looking at the regions along China's borders themselves. In this study, we examine China's relationship with North Korea by including a look at the role played by Jilin Province's border with North Korea, China's relationship with Myanmar/ Burma and Vietnam by examining at Yunnan Province and its borders with those two countries, and the role Inner Mongolia plays in shaping China's relationship with Mongolia. These are all provinces and autonomous regions that in terms of economic development lag well behind China's coastal provinces. Each also has large minority populations, with cultures and kinship ties that straddle international borders. Each province is comparable or larger in size to the country along which it borders, in terms of territory, population—or both—with leaders and local governments heavily invested for reasons that may relate as much to their own political futures as to their principles—in promoting the development and stability of their regions. Each of these provinces is geographically landlocked, elevating the importance of economic exchanges with their international neighbors in their efforts to boost local growth emulating China's national export-oriented strategy.

In pursuing its interests vis-à-vis these neighboring countries, China's policy is thus multifaceted. Local as well as national forces play significant roles in defining and implementing these specific bilateral relations. For example, China has sought to encourage economic reforms in the DPRK along the lines of its own "reform and opening," promoting Jilin's Yanbian Korean Autonomous Prefecture as a gateway, investing heavily in border infrastructure to encourage trade and investment across the border, an approach that also responds to the economic interests of landlocked Jilin. China has largely failed in this endeavor to date. Even as China has pursued this approach, North Korea has limited its economic exchanges with China and has even periodically taken the step of closing its border with China, harming Jilin's economic interests. American policymakers have asserted that China is undermining U.N. sanctions towards the DPRK, although the utility of sanctions must be questioned when North Korea believes that it can, in effect, unilaterally impose sanctions on itself as a means of pressuring its own patron. Yet, China's response to the series of security crises that have rocked the region since the Six Party Talks were suspended have frustrated the international community. From the Chinese perspective, its efforts to intensify economic interchanges with North Korea is also a form of "constructive engagement," its increased investment and trade with North Korea an effort to get North Korea to invest in regional peace and stability. From the perspective of other regional actors—the US and its allies in particular—Beijing's economic outreach to Pyongyang amid protestations of solidarity with the DPRK reads as appeasement, appeasement that has failed as yet to either serve effectively the economic interests of Jilin or to reassure or amplify its apparent leverage over its neighbor, while also doing little if anything to help lead a way out of the crisis on the world stage.

China's "sealed in blood" alliance relationship with North Korea of course has a dimension China does not share with Myanmar, where mutual goodwill is a function of a mutual perception of shared interests. Despite their shared ideological and political heritage, China's even more turbulent relationship with Vietnam may rest still more strongly on the instrumental foundation of economic exchanges. Mongolia, only independent of the last Chinese empire in 1921, is ever-wary of its massive neighbor's intentions, but it is hard to shut its ears to the siren song of China and its vast market for its raw materials. Two decades ago, as China began reshaping its relationships with the countries on its periphery amid the post-Cold war thaw; Robert Scalapino reflected that throughout history China had always given top priority to its relationships with its neighbors. While China's approach to its regional neighborhood had changed, it is possible to generalize about a "classic model" of the Chinese vision of states near its borders, the "central kingdom complex." This, Scalapino observed, has manifested itself even in the era of the PRC, pointing to the example of China's goal in its attack on Vietnam in 1979 of "punishing" the Vietnamese, an objective with a highly traditional overtone.[7] Today, many Chinese in policymaking circles or universities describe their relationships with neighboring states in traditional, Confucian terms. In explaining the Sino-North Korean relationship, for example, the DRPK is often referred to as China's "little brother." As Scalapino also reflected, it is the memory of the countries along China's edge of their role in the hierarchy of China's traditional order, which was to pay homage to the Middle Kingdom. "Bad barbarians," those who rebelled against Chinese cultural superiority, would experience the punitive face of Chinese power.[8]

A more nuanced understanding of Chinese government interests and perspectives of its own bilateral relationships with the countries along its borders is critical for the formulation of successful U.S. policies in the region. The U.S. is currently seeking to strengthen relations with Mongolia and Vietnam, while actively addressing significant human rights and security challenges presented by North Korea and Myanmar. However, it is apparent that China's interactions with those countries are a decisive factor in the success or failure of U.S. strategies; U.S. approaches must take into account the array of China's interests and objectives in promoting its interests towards those countries. Indeed, as we will show, a look at China's regional relationships through the optic of a periphery policy also suggests new opportunities for US policy that could advance American interests and influence in China and its neighboring regions in ways that can contribute constructively to the US-China relationship and regional stability.

---

7. Robert A. Scalapino "China's Relations with Its Neighbors," Proceedings of the Academy of Political Science, Vol. 38, No. 2, The China Challenge: American Policies in East Asia (1991):. 63-74.
8. Scalapino (1991)

In this study, we draw on extensive reading of the rich literature in Chinese and English on Chinese contemporary and historical security policy, its minority policy, and its management of its frontiers, open source reports in the Chinese and international media, as well as field visits to China's borders, in several provinces and autonomous regions, principally Inner Mongolia Autonomous Region, Jilin Province, and Yunnan Province. This monograph is divided into six chapters, organized as follows: Chapter 1 provides a general introduction, providing background and raising key questions and examining the relevance of this study for American policymakers; Chapter 2 examines the China-North Korea relationship; Chapter 3 examines the China-Mongolia relationship; Chapter 4 looks at the China-Vietnam relationship and the China Myanmar/ Burma relationship; and Chapter 5 concludes the study with a focus on the institutional mechanisms involved in China's management of its relationships with its territorial neighbors through its border provinces.

Among the study's key findings is that, while China certainly exerts influence over its neighboring states, China sees domestic and international security as linked along its borders. Its focus therefore is on maintaining stability along its borders and facilitating opportunities for economic exchange across the territorial borders it shares with other sovereign states. If its goals for its relationships with its neighbors are multi-pronged -- from serving its goals of domestic stability related to responding to local interests (promoting economic development within China's heavily minority frontier regions) to furthering broad national objectives, such as feeding China's enormous appetite for resources to playing to a particular bilateral situation, as in China's efforts to bolster and even open North Korea's economy as an aspect of its efforts to diminish Pyongyang's insecurity—its range of policy approaches remains limited.

Even in the context of its alliance relationship with North Korea, Beijing appears to willing to contain the potential scope of its influence by encouraging and supporting opportunities for economic exchanges, but letting local and other commercial actors determine the extent of Chinese involvement in the North Korean economy. Beijing seeks to actively encourage but does not seek to force Pyongyang to undertake the kind of political change or even economic opening that China's policies indicate it hopes North Korea will eventually embrace. One may speculate that this supports an assessment of China's foreign and security policy as still fundamentally risk averse, symptomatic both of a leadership that still considers China's domestic stability uncertain and a non-crisis policy process involving plural and decentralized actors that operates against a concentration of decision-making power (even) in the area of foreign and security policy.[9]

We would like to thank the US-China Friendship Association for its generous assistance in helping us arrange our field visits to China's border areas. We especially appreciated the bravery of our companion from that office throughout our visit to Yunnan, who conducted herself with grace and professionalism throughout the journey despite our frequent encounters with the one thing she is most

---

9. Susan Shirk, China: Fragile Superpower, (New York: Oxford, 2007); David M. Lampton, "Introduction," in David M. Lampton (ed.), The Making of Chinese Foreign and Security Policy in the Era of Reform, 1978-2000, (Stanford: Stanford University Press, 2001): 1-26; Carla Freeman, "China's Risk Averse Security Policy: China's Response to Yeongpyeong," paper presented to Chung-gang University, December 11, 2011.

terrified of dogs. We also want to thank the Smith-Richardson Foundation for making our research possible. And we are grateful to the unflagging support and understanding of our spouses who made space for our travel and then our research and writing in their own busy schedules.

......

-I-

China's Foreign and Security Policy for its Territorial Periphery

China exists in a tough regional neighborhood. The 14 states with which it shares land borders are a fractious crowd, with which the price of conflict or even bilateral tensions for China remain high. Historically, China has already borne heavy costs in blood and treasure to defend its hard won national integrity since 1949, including an estimated 900,000 casualties as a result of its engagement in Korea, bloody conflicts with India and Russia over border disputes that contributed to China's international isolation with its costly autarchic economic policies, and outright war to low-level border conflicts Vietnam from 1979 through the late 1980s. Today, while China and its neighbors have largely resolved their differences, the countries on China's immediate borders remain a difficult bunch. They include among them three established nuclear powers, two international pariahs, and other countries fraught with the gamut of social and economic challenges, relatively newly won independence, uncertain political futures, and the presence of groups with ties to international terrorism.

However difficult these countries are, nearly all have formed important economic partnerships with China. As China has sought to sustain its growth, it has become a major importer of natural resources from among the resource-endowed countries in its regional neighborhood, with which it has also engaged in an increasingly high volume of two-way trade. China's economic exchanges with territorially contiguous states have taken place not only at the national level, but between neighboring states and the provinces and autonomous regions located on China's territorial edge, which, in the context of China's heavily decentralized approach to economic development, have sought to expand economic exchanges across their international borders. These exchanges have become progressively more important sources of economic activity within China's still economically struggling, often landlocked provinces and subprovincial regions on the border. Even as members of the international community pressure China to "act responsibly" by censuring and sanctioning such neighbors as North Korea or Myanmar, China's growing ties with its neighbors and these subnational linkages make this not only economically but politically difficult as well given the extensive investment of localities in these cross-border relationships.

At the same time, as China's relative power grows within its regional neighborhood, managing its relations with its neighbors has become an increasingly significant dimension of its foreign policy. As will be discussed below, China's interests vis-à-vis its neighbors have evolved over the past decades as its economy and capabilities have grown and the international and regional environment has also changed. China's relations with its supersize neighbors, India and Russia, have their own complexities as they have developed for the better in the past two decades, but bilateral interactions are constrained by mutual caution given their history of conflict, military might as well as nuclear capabilities.

Absent these constraints, China has been able to deepen its ties more easily with most of the smaller states in the region, through trade, and, related to this, through different types of flows across borders. These ties have become important not only in supporting China's economic development and energy security goals; they have also brought China and Chinese into an encounter with the many political, economic and social changes underway in these smaller countries across their borders. As China confronts the security implications of these changes, which include among them rising Muslim fundamentalism, potential nuclear proliferation, competition for national energy resources, and a sustained American presence on its doorstep, managing its relations with these neighbors to safeguard its national interests has also become a new challenge for Beijing. China has addressed this challenge through a variety of approaches and mechanisms that draw upon a range of political and economic resources.

Good Neighbor Policy

Since China committed itself to a policy of "economic reform and opening" thirty years ago, an important aim of its foreign policy has been to seek to improve the chances for sustained peace and stability within its regional neighborhood in the interest of its own development. In the early 1980s, China sought to cultivate better relations with countries on its periphery to mitigate the threats along its borders that had been major sources of international insecurity throughout the Cold War period. Even before the Soviet collapse, China's leaders decided to set aside ideological differences in diplomatic relations with neighboring states in an effort to forge new ties with them without reference to which "camp" – the US or USSR – they were in. This approach enabled China to begin building new relationships with India and South Korea, and allowed it to negotiate normal relations with Mongolia.

After 1989 and Tiananmen, China moved rapidly to further improve its bilateral relationships with the countries on its borders and in the region. While the US and other western countries imposed economic sanctions on China after June 4, its neighbors remained generally friendly. Talk of "Asian values" in the human rights sphere, as well as the "East Asian economic model" supported improved relations between China and countries in the region.[10] At the same time, without the Soviet menace, troops along China's northern border could be drawn down and China could focus on modernizing its military, including retraining and retooling its forces for their more targeted use to contend with limited threats along its borders.[11]

In the early 2000s, China's "good neighbor policy" took on a new dimension. The American response to the 9/11 attack brought the United States to China's doorstep as never before. Its military presence and growing ties to Central Asian states raised many concerns in Beijing over the implications for China's western autonomous regions as well as broader strategic worries about an American encirclement of China. China sought to improve its own ties with Central Asian countries. It deepened its economic presence there and worked to strengthen the Shanghai Cooperation Organization (SCO), a regional grouping including China, Russia and Central Asian states along with regional observers then focused on regional security and border management issues, including adopting a zero-

---

10. Closely drawn from Suisheng Zhao, "China Rising: Geo-Strategic Thrust and Diplomatic Engagement," in Suisheng Zhao (ed.), China-U.S. Relations Transformed: Perspectives and Strategic Interactions (Routledge, UK: 2008): 32-34.
11. Paul H. B. Godwin, "From Continent to Periphery: PLA Doctrine, Strategy and Capabilities Towards 2000," The China Quarterly, No. 146, (June,1996): 464-487.

tolerance policy on Islamist and separatist policies. As the 2000s moved forward, China's policy formulations suggested its "good neighbor" approach had become one dimension among many efforts to reassure its regional neighborhood that its rise was an opportunity not a threat.[12] Broadly stated, throughout much of the reform period, China's policy aims within its regional neighborhood were twofold: to engender a positive and stable regional environment conducive to its own development; and to reassure countries in the region that the effects of its rising power on their interests will be benign or even beneficial.

In more recent years, however, China's objectives for its role in its neighborhood have shifted. The growing importance of imports of resources, raw materials and increasingly energy in China's interactions with its neighbors has added a more explicit economic and energy dimension to China's calculations vis à vis its relationships with contiguous states. This is evident in the role played by China's most senior leaders, who are increasingly seen inking deals in national capitals around the region, or celebrating plans for greater "investment cooperation" with their neighborhood counterparts in Beijing. Bilateral agreements, such as the China-Kazakhstan Cooperative Commission, serve as frameworks for cooperation in economic and natural resources development, as well international security. Yunnan and Guangxi were among the earliest regions to launch pilot projects for cross-border RMB trade with ASEAN, pilots soon extended to more

---

12. Shulan Ye, 5-6.

than a dozen, autonomous regions, provinces and cities, including Inner Mongolia and Liaoning.[13]

China has also sought to expand military cooperation with its neighbors. This may take the form of high-level military exchanges, and arms and military equipment sales but also often is manifest in confidence-building activities along shared borders. Public security cooperation is also an important dimension of most of these cross-border relationships, as in the agreement to jointly combat human trafficking signed between China and Vietnam in 2010.[14]

China has also sought to engage its neighbors in multilateral fora at the regional level. China's role in the SCO, ASEAN + 3 and the East Asia Summit, and the Six Party process—all involving its neighbors or near neighbors—is well studied. It has also been part of subregional groups, most notably Greater Mekong Subregion and the Greater Tumen Initiative, as well as the proposed "Kunming Initiative," in which, as will be discussed, Chinese border provinces play leading roles.

---

13. Administrative rules for the Pilot Program for the Settlement of Cross-border of Trade Transactions ("Rules") was promulgated by the People's Bank of China (PBC), the Ministry of Finance (MOF), the Ministry of Commerce (MOC), the General Administration of Customs (GAC), the State Administration of Tax (SAT), and the China Bank Regulatory Commission (CBRC), which marked the formal implementation of the pilot scheme of RMB settlement of cross-border trade transactions in early July 2009. Shanghai, Guangzhou, Shenzhen, Zhuhai, and Dongguan were the first pilot cities, and Hong Kong, Macao and ASEAN countries were the first overseas pilot regions, see Lian Lian, " RMB Settlement of Cross-Border Transactions.
14. Vietnam, China ink Human Trafficking Combat Agreement, Vietnam Plus, September 10, 2010, available at http://www.dztimes.net/post/politics/vietnam china-ink-human-trafficking-combat-agreement.aspx.

China's Provinces and Local Leaders in Border Policy

This leads us to a critical but under-recognized cross-border and local dimension of China's relationships with its neighbors. China's border provinces, autonomous regions and local administrative entities along China's territorial edges are not passive actors in China's relations with contiguous states. The continual interactions with neighboring states along their borders influence the broader bilateral dynamic between China and these neighbors. In addition, they not only play an important role in interpreting central policies, but also in shaping the direction and objectives of policies to reflect their own parochial interests and concerns, as well as their own historical and cultural relationships with their international neighbors.

The devolution of considerable decision-making authority to subnational authorities in the economic management of local administrative regions has been a feature of China's post-Mao reforms. Certainly centrally-set policy goals and targets are used to guide decision making at the local level, with the promotion prospects of local cadres closely tied to success or failure in meeting centrally-determined objectives. The process of determining these objectives, including the allocation of fiscal and other resources to localities, however, allows for considerable bargaining on the part of the powerful provincial Party secretary at the apex of the provincial governance structure. They have influence emanating from their important representation in China's most powerful political institutions, such as the Central Committee, as well as their personal networks within China's senior leadership. Currently, provincial and provincial-level city leaders hold 2 of the 9 PSC seats and 10 of the 25 Politburo seats.15 Provincial leaders also hold the

15. Linda Jakobson and Dean Knox, "New Foreign Policy Actors in China," SIPRI Policy Paper No. 26, September 2010: 32, available at http://books.sipri.org/files/PP/SIPRIPP 26.pdf.

power to appoint leaders for subprovincial administrative entities, interpret central objectives for national development for their province and set policy agendas and budget allocations accordingly. Through provincial foreign affairs offices, a provincial-level "leading group" comprising senior provincial officials, and other provincial-level offices, such as the provincial departments of commerce and other entities, such as "friendship associations," "people's associations," and other semi-governmental groups, such as "sub-councils" and provincial chapters of the China Council for the Promotion of International Trade, provincial-level leaders manage and promote provincial interests overseas.[16] Provincial heads represent their provinces abroad, often meeting with the leaders of the states they visit.[17] The heads of Chinese provinces thus have penultimate authority over the management of economic development, including foreign economic relations, in geographic areas and for populations that may be as large as or larger than states across their international borders.[18]

---

16. "Statutes of the Chinese People's Association for Friendship with Foreign Countries," The Chinese People's Association for Friendship with Foreign Countries: (http://www.cpaffc.org.cn/yszz/detaile.php?subid=662&id=303); see also Peter T.Y. Cheung and James T.H. Tang, "The External Relations of Chinese Provinces," in David M. Lampton (ed.), The Making of Chinese Foreign and Security Policy in the Era of Reform, (Stanford: Stanford University Press, 2001): 91-120.
17. See for example, "Yunnan Party Leader Welcomed to Vietnam," Nhan Dan on-line, November 26, 2010: http://www.nhandan.com.vn/cmlink/nhandan-online/homepage/politics/external-relations/yunnan-party-leader-welcomed-to-vietnam-1.275613#20r96AxFRo9p.
18. See for example David M. Lampton, ,"A Plum for a Peach: Bargaining, Interest, and Bureaucratic Politics," in Kenneth G. Lieberthal and David M. Lampton, (eds.), Bureaucracy, Politics, and Decision Making in Post-Mao China, (Berkeley: University of California Press, 1992):

Provincial authorities, whose measure of success as leaders is heavily weighted toward the growth rates they produce within their administrative jurisdictions, are eager to develop their provinces' economic exchanges with countries across the border. Expanding opportunities for cross-border trade and investment is seen as an important way to boost local growth. In addition, from the local perspective, not only are cross-border flows of ethnic groups that share kinship and cultural ties an historical norm, such ties between groups like Uyghur's, Mongols, Koreans, Zhuang, Dai or Yi spanning China's borders between Xinjiang and Kyrgyzstan, Inner Mongolia and Mongolia, Jilin and North Korea, and Yunnan and Vietnam represent a potential competitive advantage in vying for access to resources and markets in China's neighboring states. Local leaders in border areas also assess that their own regions, as bridges to these countries along China's periphery have become more important to China's economic and energy security as well, must be all the more consequential to China's development strategy. As importantly, provincial-level leaders are fundamentally responsible for stability within their provinces. Successful management of the Kokang refugee crisis in 2009 left Yunnan's long-governing Party secretary Bai Enpei in place; Wang Lequan, Xinjiang's Party secretary for more than 15 years, was recalled to Beijing and demoted after ethnic violence struck Xinjiang.[19]

Homeland Security and Foreign Policy

For Beijing, there is no doubt that it sees the role of its border provinces as vital to its economic relationships around its neighborhood as well as farther afield. At the

---

19. Katherine Simpson,"'King of Xinjiang' Wang Lequan Replaced by Man with "a Spirit of Creative Thought,"Shanghailist, available at http://shanghaiist.com/2010/04/26/xinjiang-wang-lequan-replaced.php.

same, however, cross-border links are viewed with wariness as well-known potential pathways to the emergence of transnational problems. These include the emergence of border-spanning ethno-nationalism that could challenge China's nation-building enterprise, particularly given the fragility of many of its neighboring states. In this context, a porous border and cross-border flows may inject an ambiguous intimacy to the bilateral relationship. China's border regions remain under developed and abut countries with weak governance and internal security capacity, some in the throes of internal conflict, or experiencing endemic poverty. Some of these border states may be incubators of extremism and international terrorism, or such illicit activities as drug and human trafficking that also often serve as sources of revenue to fund these movements. Border states may also be repositories for violent crime and disease, affecting China's side of the border. Failed or pariah states risk embroiling China in bigger political or economic problems that spill across the border, such as the crisis following Naypiytaw's attacks on Kokang territory along the Yunnan frontier, which resulted in a flood of more than 35,000 refugees into Chinese border towns in 2009. The related deaths and injuries of Chinese in the border area and the loss of property by those Chinese who had emigrated into Myanmar to do business led to calls by some Chinese citizens for Beijing to intervene across the border to protect the ethnically Chinese Kokang. When these fragile states become threats to global stability or perpetrators of human rights abuses, China is unhappy that they may be drawn into international debates linking its commercial relationship with the domestic failings of these sovereign states.

Instability and ethnic unrest on the China side of the border worry Beijing on many levels; domestic unrest indicates the failure of domestic minority and development policy in these strategically sensitive regions, challenging a basic principle in Beijing's contemporary claims to political legitimacy: that of delivering national stability to enable a prosperous society. Such unrest also stirs old fears of vulnerability, recalling one of the ancient "thirty-six strategems" often referred to by Chinese thinkers about Chinese security—in part because it resonates so clearly with China's 19th and early 20th century history—that of "looting a burning house (chenhuodajia)," or the idea that a country experiencing internal conflicts is ripest for external interference. Furthermore, such ethnic strife represents additional potential challenges for China's foreign relations. For instance, China's actions to suppress unrest on its side of the border imperil vital international relationships, such as the risk that China's otherwise excellent relationship with the Muslim world (and heavy dependence on oil from sources with predominantly Muslim populations) could be compromised by its actions in Xinjiang.

China's perception of its border regions as valuable, but also both vulnerable and threatening to its geographic core, has deep roots in its history. In imperial times, these zones were by definition new territory for the Chinese empire, providing space for an expanding Han population at different times in history, but also providing a source of new resources, from agricultural land on which to increase food production, to forest and mineral resources.[20] During China's imperial period, these frontier zones often resisted control by the Chinese imperium; even when officially integrated into China's imperial geography, they periodically aligned with

20. James A. Millward, "New Perspectives on the Qing Frontier," in Gail Hershatter, Emily Honig, Jonathan N. Lipman, and Randall Stross (eds.), Remapping China: Fissures in Historical Terrain, (Stanford, 1996): 124; Naomi Standen, "Raiding and Frontier Society in the Five Dynasties," in Nicola Di Cosma and Don J. Wyatt, Political Frontier, Ethnic Boundaries, and Human Geography in Chinese History, (Routledge,, Curzon, 2003): 174-175.

nomadic populations to the North and West to challenge Chinese rule. During the era of European-led imperialism, China's political weakness and faltering hold over these regions and, the sheer geographic distance of its frontier from the Chinese capital made its periphery susceptible to capture by the Russians, British, and Japanese. Nor have China's leaders today forgotten the more recent role played by the American CIA with Indian complicity in Tibet in the middle of the last century.

The post-9/11 US military engagements on its doorsteps have only elevated China's sense of insecurity. Among Chinese concerns: the American presence in the region is perceived as more likely contributing to intensifying jihadist activity than to diminishing it, with the concomitant concern that this could raise the influence of militant Islam among Chinese Muslims, especially within the Uyghur population in Xinjiang.[21] Similarly, China's border neuralgia is reinforced by latent fears of encirclement by the United States and its allies, periodically aggravated by everything from American arms sales to Taiwan, presidential tête à têtes with the Dalai Lama, to the US handling of the 2010 Cheonan incident.

Domestic and international security interests are thus interwoven both in the geographic and policy space of China's border regions. Within China, Beijing seeks both to tighten control over and better integrate its former imperial frontiers—still referred to as "outer" as distinct from "inner" China—into the Chinese heartland. At the same time, as China seeks to sustain its national economic development

21. See discussion in Michael Swaine, "China and the 'Af-Pak" Issue," China Leadership Monitor, (2010.31): (http://www.hoover.org/publications/china-leadership-monitor/article/5274): especially pp. 3-4 and related notes.

by tapping available resources both inside and beyond China's borders to fuel its growth it also wants to secure access to these resources, by seeking to ensure stability along its periphery, beyond as well as within its borders. Instability in contiguous regions can spill across boundaries to disrupt conditions within China. In *The Science of Military Strategy,* the first English-language volume on strategy by the People's Liberation Army published in 2005, the "[correct] handling [of]... the outward screening effect of frontiers and (emphasis added) opening up" is considered of "vital importance" to both "stabilization" and the "balance" of China's "geo-strategic relationship with neighboring states."[22]

China has used a number of different approaches aimed at mitigating insecurity within its domestic periphery. China's central government has been prepared to ensure security in these regions through hard tactics. The People's Armed Police (PAP), often confused in the western media with China's military, were used to restore quiescence after the riots in Lhasa and Urumqi in 2008 and 2009 respectively. Provincial civilian authorities have authority over PAP involved in border patrol, internal security, as well as other emergency units.[23] China's sophisticated Domestic Security Department within Ministry of Public Security, which oversees provincial and subprovincial police departments, also operates a network of propaganda and intelligence personnel in border regions, as it does throughout China, which monitors and manages any perceived threats to

22. Peng Guangqian, Yao Youzhi, (eds.), The Science of Military Strategy, (Beijing, Military Science Publishing House, 2005): 66.
23. Drew Thompson and Carla Freeman, "Flood Across the Border: China's Disaster Relief Operations and Potential Response to a North Korean Refugee Crisis, US-Korea Institute and The Nixon Center (2009): 48.

security. It coordinates its intelligence operations with China's Ministry of State Security, which has an important role in domestic counterintelligence as well as foreign intelligence operations.[24]

China has led with a "soft" approach to managing its border regions, however, effectively accelerating a process of assimilation of these regions through state-led financing for economic development. This has proved far more effective in knitting these former frontier areas to the rest of China than earlier government policies, such as those of state-led resettlement of Han Chinese in minority region areas. In Xinjiang, the quasi-military Xinjiang Production and Construction Corp (XPCC) explicitly combines development and security. The security objectives of other projects are more oblique. The "Western Development Program" (WDP) is the most ambitious of such relatively recent programs. Launched in 1999, the WDP was a response in part to a perception that the widening economic gap between its coast and hinterland represented a potential threat to national unity, particularly since many of the regions that were lagging farthest behind were heavily populated by ethnic minorities. China's border provinces and autonomous regions of Guangxi, Yunnan, Tibet, Xinjiang, Gansu, Inner Mongolia, Heilongjiang and Jilin include some of China's poorest regions. Linked to the WDP "a "Program to Develop Border Areas and Enrich the Lives of the People Living There," or more simply termed the "Prosperous Borders, Wealthy Minorities" program (PBWM) project was enacted in 2000 by the Central Committee of the Communist Party of China (CPC). Led by the State Ethnic Affairs Commission, the National Development and Reform Commission (NDRC) and the Ministry of Finance, the project was piloted with central

---

24. Nicholas Eftimiades, Chinese Intelligence Operations, (United States, Reed Business Information, Inc., 1994).

funding in nine border counties in 2000 and expanded to 17 the following year. By 2008, 120 counties were receiving funds under the scheme. By 2009, every county on China's border, including 58 units in the Xinjiang Production and Construction Corps, were enrolled. In 2000, RMB15 million was allocated to PBWM projects. By 2009, RMB4.84 billion was spent. By the government's calculation, over 190,000 square kilometers of territory and 21 million people have benefitted from the program.[25] This aligns with World Bank estimates that suggest that about 40% of China's poverty alleviation funding has gone toward China's five minority autonomous regions and its three provinces with the largest minority populations.[26]

The focus of these projects has been on infrastructure development, tying these regions into China's national transportation networks. Thousands of kilometers of new highways have been constructed since the program was launched; travelers from Shanghai can now make the 4400 kilometer journey to Lhasa by train, and new airports in major cities in these regions link them to Beijing and other cities along China's coast. Again, this can be seen as China weaving these regions more intricately into "inner China," also indirectly facilitating Han in-migration along with regional economic integration.

In addition to transportation infrastructure, priorities for the 2006-2010 "11th Five Year Plan" period also included building facilities in administrative villages, replacing thatched roof buildings, improving access to drinking water, strengthening the rural power grid and ecological protection projects. Along with ramping up investment

25. "," , January 7, 2010. http://news.xinhuanet.com/theory/2010-01/07/content_12768592.htm
26. Information provided by team member of the World Bank's "Poor Rural Communities Development Project" (estimates from 2005).

in infrastructure, expected out comes of the program include poverty reduction and increasing incomes, and, importantly, developing border trade and regional economic cooperation.

But the objectives for the program go beyond spurring local development. The PBWM program's stated objectives are to "strengthen national unity and safeguard stability in border areas," aiming to achieve, "wealthy people, happy borders, a strong country, and harmonious and friendly neighbors [mulin] (emphasis added)."[27] In other words, these policies are seen as promoting stability (and development) not only on Chinese territory, but across the border as well, where it is expected that these new opportunities will garner China (and China's local government) good will and influence in communities on the opposite side. To enable this "win-win" economic relationship in border regions, local governments have implemented various policies approved by the central government to encourage border trade and investment. Duties are waived for locals living within 20-30 kilometers of the border (with the precise distance depending on the region) on goods up to a certain value (usually RMB 3,000). Local immigration officials on both sides of many border crossings have the authority to issue "border resident passes" (bianmin churu jingtong xingzheng) which allow border residents to cross the border freely, subjected only to a cursory inspection and a quick stamp in their booklet.

Enabling this managed cross-border economic interaction requires a border control infrastructure. Along some borders, such as North Korea and Myanmar, neighboring countries have not invested significantly in developing a

---

27. ,"June 16, 2007: The Central People's Government of the People's Republic of China, (http://www1.www.gov.cn/zwgk/2007-06/15/content_650280.htm).

border management infrastructure as sophisticated as that of China's. Indeed, some reports suggest that along some borders, there is an assumption that China's capacity to control its borders is so strong that such investments would be redundant. [28] This contrasts with the situation between Chinese border provinces or autonomous regions and a number of other states. For example, Vietnam has also set up facilities at key border ports to manage border trade and the daily inflows and outflows of the people who conduct it.

In recent years, China has also come far toward completing a technologically sophisticated "border information integration system," launched nearly a decade ago beginning with Xinjiang, inner Mongolia and Yunnan, the provinces and autonomous regions with the longest land borders.[29] In addition, it has invested significantly in computerizing its border control for people entering and leaving China. Along with this technology, it has also invested in constructing new border port structures. Today, border crossings on the Chinese side are typically marked by large archways, known as "country doors" (guomen) that appear designed to impress visitors, and that are often destinations for Chinese tourists. The archways are often functional as well, containing administrative offices for the various government bureaus tasked with controlling border crossings—the port office, health and quarantine officials, customs, and the people's armed police—and in some cases also housing immigration check points as well.

---

28. Hayder Mili and Jacob Townsend, "Precursor Control on Central Asia's Borders with China," United Nations Office on Drugs and Crime, Regional Office for Central Asia, (2006): (http://www.unodc.org/documents/afghanistan//Precursor_Control/PrecursorRep.pdf.)
29. "Electronic Border Shield being built in China," China-Defense-Mashup, August 23, 2008: (http://www.china-defense-mashup.com/electronic border-shield-being-built-in-china.html).

However, it is the infrastructure set back from the "country door" gateway that is the real catalyst for trade and development. Small inland ports feature "border markets" where citizens from both sides can rent stalls and sell goods. Larger border crossings feature "economic zones" with sizeable, permanent markets, stores and offices are located, as well as warehouses, truck parks and cargo transfer areas. Ruili along China's border with Myanmar and Hekou along its border with Vietnam are two such border cities with robust border cooperation zones; zones are also under development in Inner Mongolia's Erlian and along the North Korean border at Dandong and Tumen, for example.[30]

China's "prosperous and secure" border crossings have a number of common features. Interestingly, the degree of stability in the neighboring state does not appear to be a limiting factor. For instance, the border markets at the Ruili-Muse crossing between Yunnan and Myanmar are thriving, despite the economic and political conditions within Myanmar. Regardless of challenges in dealing with their counterparts, Chinese officials seek to develop commerce and ensure stability in their border jurisdictions by maintaining regular contact between foreign affairs officers, immigration officers, public health authorities and security personnel from both sides of the borders. These contacts are conducted on regular, scheduled cycles as well as via ad hoc arrangements.

Despite the economic benefits associated with trade

---

30. Robert L. Wallach, "Harmonizing Border Development of Southeast Gobi, Mongolia & Inner Mongolia Autonomous Region, People's Republic of China, "Development of Regional Cooperation Programs for Mongolia and the People's Republic of China, Asian Development Bank (June 2009): (www.adb.org/Documents/Reports/Consultant/.../42184-08-MON-TACR.pdf).

through relatively porous borders, local Chinese officials are also concerned about the potential hazards associated with border exchanges. Striking the right balance between openness and security is a difficult task for local officials in border regions, particularly in areas where cross-border relations are tense or where insecurity dominates on one side. Chinese officials identify the most significant non-traditional security threats as the problem of illegal "over-stayers," smuggling and cross-border crime. These challenges are confronted on the Chinese-side comprehensively in a whole-of-government approach. At the border-line itself, guards and civilian officials staff check points. Approximately 25 kilometers from the border-line, a "second line" of security is maintained by public security border guards who limit access to and from border areas. Civilian authorities manage citizens from neighboring states in this zone, permitting them to engage in economic activities. Immigration officials control border passes. Health and quarantine officials staff check-points to screen for infectious diseases, while commerce officials establish and license border markets where citizens from both sides can conduct business.

Local officials are also conscious that China's rise has also increased concerns by its neighbors even at the local level about China's strategic intent. Not long ago, China's border regions were zones of military tension; trust building across some borders remains a work in progress. As one local Chinese official on the border with Burma acknowledging the challenges of reassuring China's smaller neighbors about the impact of its growing power commented, attributing the quote to Ne Win, "When the elephant dances, the grass gets trampled."[31] Yunnan authorities are acutely aware of this issue with respect to the relationship with their Vietnamese counterparts, especially in the security sector.

---

31. Authors' interview, Yunnan 2010.

With memories of the 1979 war and 1984-86 border clashes still in mind, they identify trust building between the two-sides' security forces as a particularly important task. Today, Chinese authorities notify their Vietnamese counterparts in advance of planned patrols by armed police and military units. In some cases, security forces from both sides conduct simultaneous or joint patrols along the border to maintain security and ensure that border markers have not been moved. A Chinese official, who had worked at one border crossing for a dozen years, described the social activities that border guards from the Chinese and Vietnamese sides engaged in, recounting how they frequently ate (and drank) together and enjoyed good personal, as well as professional relationships.[32]

From China's Border Policies to US Interests

At the height of Ming power, imperial officials debated the best strategies to promote China's security from the nomads and other peoples at the edges of the empire. Some felt a military approach, characterized by the liberal use of force and strict limits on trade—a coercive pacification strategy in effect—was necessary to protect China's core from the nomadic peoples who challenged imperial rule. Others saw a commercially-oriented policy in the tradition of the "loose rein" system (jimizhi) as the most effective approach to preventing aggression from nomadic peoples. This approach ultimately prevailed, flourishing alongside a strengthened Great Wall, so that while borders were drawn more firmly, a policy enabling the flows of goods and traders across borders also linked China's interior to the economic actors along and well beyond China's frontier.

In the wake of the Qing conquest and its military expansion, the Qing answered the question of a "loose or tight" approach to frontier management with its own

32. Authors' interviews 2010.

formula, giving preference to trade to manage Central Asians and other borderland peoples, but with commercial exchanges with neighbors unequivocally categorized as a "national security issue" to be closely managed by the state. Han Chinese relied on loans from Qing officials to engage in trade with Mongols and other non-Han peoples, creating a web of debt relations that bound neighboring non-Han elites to the Chinese state. When debt relations failed to prevent the emergence of perceived threats to Qing security from its frontier, the Qing was prepared to apply coercive or punitive methods to quash potential challenges.[33] Notably, as legal scholar R. Randle Edwards has argued, this strategy was accompanied by a highly regulated and relatively centralized border control system aimed at managing the flow of goods and people across Qing imperial borders, territorial borders that the imperial court sought to delimit in its relations with neighboring countries.[34]

Parallels between contemporary and historical debates among Chinese policy makers cannot of course be deterministically drawn to understand contemporary Chinese thinking about its foreign policy and security with neighboring countries. Nonetheless, today's Chinese policy makers confront similar dilemmas as the security objectives along their borders have become increasingly complex and multilayered. On one level, these include ensuring that security threats affecting China do not develop within the sovereign states contiguous to Chinese territory. On another, they involve preventing problems on

33. Peter Perdue, "Coercion and Commerce on Two Chinese Frontiers," in Nicola Di Cosmo (ed.), Military Culture in Imperial China, (Cambridge: Harvard University Press, 2009): 325-334.
34. R. Randle Edwards, "Imperial China's Border Control Law," Journal of Chinese Legal Studies (Vol 1.1 Spring 1987).

China's side of the border that could be amplified through interactions with groups outside China's borders. On yet another, they include creating an enabling environment for China's neighbors to continue to play their important roles in China's economic and energy security. On the Chinese side of the border, this involves ensuring stability in its own border regions to facilitate flows of resources through China's border zones into China's interior. Across China's borders and within neighboring states, this means securing access to these resources.

How is China seeking to achieve these goals today? Is a "loose rein" and fundamentally commercial approach the way it is "managing" neighborly relations with the idea that interdependence fosters stability? Or does its practice suggest that it is pursuing a deliberate state directed strategy to create dependencies on it on the part of its neighbors? An important difference between the imperial and contemporary context is that Chinese policy makers now confront far better organized and, if potentially more lethal, also generally more predictable actors along its borders, including both China's own administrative entities and the states that are its neighbors. Although, as noted, the leaders of China's own administrative regions play effective bargaining roles within the policy process, this does not signify that political discipline within China is weak; an effective nomenklatura system among other political tools ensure that leaders at levels of authority that have influence on policy are heavily invested in political success within the system. Even so, Xinjiang and Tibet have tested the capacity of even the most seasoned leaders to manage their populations.[35] Other minority areas along China's borders have also summoned up the specter of

35. Hu Jintao served as Party Regional Committee Secretary of Tibet from 1988-1992, where he declare martial law in March 1989 amid widening protests.

threats to Chinese sovereignty, including the deepening ties between the Zhuang and other Kam-Thai speaking people on the Vietnam border, and a growing push for official recognition by other Chinese ethnic groups, including the Manchus—a group long considered culturally assimilated within China—concentrated in Liaoning.[36]

This raises additional questions about China's periphery policy. Is insecurity a feature common to China's perception of all of its border regions; are there some regions where the local population is seen as more or less a threat to China's national security? Are the regions in which China's government feels less secure also places where it is therefore more intrusive and, if so, how? To what extent are the parochial interests of China's border regions themselves reflected in China's policy toward neighboring states? How does China's approach to Mongolia or Vietnam, the former a steadily developing, relatively stable democracy, and the latter an authoritarian and certain politically effective state, differ from China's approach to its relations with neighboring countries with more fragile political circumstances, such as North Korea or Myanmar? Or are there other predominant drivers, such as neighboring states' own foreign or security policies within the region, including their ties or lack thereof to the United States, and their perceived impact on China's interests?

The insights into these questions this monograph seeks to provide are significant for US policy and policymakers. It is clear that, as discussed above, the regional presence of the United States has complicated China's perception of security along its borders. Continued U.S. support for exile groups, particularly U.S. government funding

36. Dru C. Gladney, Dislocating China: Reflections on Muslims, Minorities and Other Subaltern Subjects (London, C. Hurst & Co. Publishers, 2004): 18-20.

channeled through NGOs, contributes to Chinese distrust of U.S. intentions towards it. The restrictions on civil society constrain groups from participating in policy making or citizen oversight, potentially amplifying pent up frustration and dissatisfaction by minorities and the perception by many in the U.S., often incorrectly, that human rights abuses are widespread in many minority autonomous regions. Recent regulations requiring stricter oversight of foreign funding received by NGOs are an indication of the government's concerns about expanding foreign influence. However, minority-Han tensions and concerns about NGOs are not evenly distributed, evidenced by the relatively vibrant civil society and relaxed political atmosphere in some regions, such as Yunnan province for example. For China, U.S. attention and involvement in and in regions contiguous to many minority regions represents much more than a difference over the interpretation of individual or community rights, but a direct threat to China's core interests, in a space where China feels particularly insecure.

In addition, China's views toward the U.S. role in the Western Pacific, Central Asia, and deepening American relationships with Mongolia, Vietnam and India appears to be moving from one of ambivalence toward a position that the US presence is undesirable, aimed inexorably at damaging Chinese interests, rather than enabling China's development. Chinese strategists and policy-makers are increasingly quick to identify U.S. support for Tibetan and Xinjiang exile groups, in addition to U.S. security guarantees to Taiwan and U.S. bases in Central Asia, as part of a concerted strategy to weaken and contain China and ultimately constrain what they see as its inevitable rise. Rear Adm. Guan Youfei's invective toward US strategic intent at the May 2010 Shangri-la Dialogue encapsulated the sense shared by some in Chinese political and military circles that, rather than reflecting an acknowledgment of China's renewed capabilities, US pressure to cooperate or exercise leadership in various international security areas, from Korea to Iran to climate change is designed to trap China within a tangle of debilitating commitments within its region and beyond.[37]

Understanding how Beijing is approaching the management of its relationships with its regional neighbors offers insights into how China is shaping its strategic approach on its territorial edge. Examining China's approach to its "near abroad" that analyzes these questions from the perspective of a periphery policy allows insights into how China sees its regional security from the inside out, insights that enabling a more nuanced response on the part of the United States to China's policies in the region.

---

37. John Pomfret, "The Shangri-la Dialogue," Washington Post, June 8, 2010, available at http://www.iiss.org/whats-new/iiss-in-the-press/june-2010/in-chinese-admirals-outburst-a-lingering-distrust-of-us/.

-II-

Uncertain Engagement: China and North Korea

Hu said that at present, China and the DPRK are increasing vigorous exchange and cooperation in various fields, among various departments and between provinces along the borders..."

Paintings of Kim Il-Sung on the North Korean side of a bridge crossing Tumen River[38]

---

38. Author's photo. Unless otherwise indicated, all photos are the author's copyright.

"Kim said that the northeastern part of China is the place where DPRK-China friendship began."

"Hu Jintao Holds Talks with Kim Jong-Il in Changchun," PRC, Ministry of Foreign Affairs, August 20, 2010.

China has a 1400 km long border with North Korea that for most of its length follows the flow of the Yalu and Tumen Rivers from their origins at Baitoushan (Mt. Paektu), dividing Liaoning and Jilin provinces from North Korea. The border has been a focal point of China's relationship with the Korean peninsula from imperial days when China sought to establish a border with its then Choson neighbor, even then seeking to mamigration into its territory from the peninsula.[39] The struggle against "US aggression" in the Korean War may have forged Sino-DPRK friendship in blood," but the border remained an object of Conflict between the two sides. Allthough China and North Korea signed a military alliance in 1961 followed by a border treaty a few years later, they reported engaged in border skirmishes in the late 1960s, [40] at a time when they were also at ideological odds over the Soviet invasion of Czechoslovakia. Regular border trade between the two sides resumed only in 1982.

Amid the Cold War politics of the peninsula that continue to persist, however, the two countries have sought to manage their bilateral tensions behind a façade of solidarity. Most recently, this has been severely tested by North Korea's

---

39. See for example Andre Schmid on the Qing-Choson frontier in Andre Schmid, "Tributary Relations and the Qing-Choson Frontier on Mount Paektu," in Diana Lary (ed.), The Chinese State at the Borders, (Vancouver, UBC Press, 2007): 126-150.
40. Daniel Gomez Pinilla, "Border Disputes between China and North Korea,"China Perspectives, Vol. 52 (2004), available at http://chinaperspectives.revues.org/806?&id=806.

nuclear ambitions. Beijing has stood with the international community in condemning its ally for its nuclear tests, but it has taken what a US Congressional memorandum criticized as a "minimalist[41] approach to implementing sanctions in North Korea,"criticism widely echoed in the international community. China has continued to provide food aid to North Korea and to find opportunities to expand its economic relationship with its neighbor.

China's long border with North Korea is the leading factor in this economic engagement. Security concerns related to the border loom large in China's calculation. Mitigating the China's long border with North Korea is the leading factor in this economic engagement. Security concerns related to the border loom large in China's calculation. Mitigating threat of a full-fledged economic collapse in North Korea is certainly one important aim Offering symbolic reassurance of friendship toward Pyongyang is another. But, as a look at Chinese actions makes clear, deepening linkages between China and North Korea across the border to encourage Pyongyang to move in the direction of a more open and trade oriented economy is a key objective. There is certainly an opportunistic dimension to this--the acquisition by Chinese owned firms of some resource concessions and expanded port access has taken place as most of North Korea's other economic relationships, including with South Korea have deteriorated. But China has long sought to moderate North Korean behavior by weaving its economy into its own economic activity, and so into the regional economy, thus giving it a greater stake in regional stability. Following the collapse of the Six Party Talks, China's frenetic inking of investment deals and infrastructure projects to better connect neighboring Chinese and North Korean provinces has become nothing less than China's North Korean strategy. Yet, the strategy

---

41. Congressional Research Service Memorandum: "Implementation of UN Security Council Resolution 1874," October 8, 2010, available at http://lugar.senate.gov/issues/foreign/reports/NKoreaCRSReport.pdf

is tempered by limited interest by Chinese companies in taking on the risk involved in doing business in North Korea's business-unfriendly environment.

China's border provinces, especially Jilin and the subprovincial localities within the province, principally the province's Yanbian Korean Autonomous prefecture, have been leading actors in this "constructive engagement" strategy by China toward North Korea. They are both the primary victims of North Korean fragility, and the primary beneficiaries of Beijing's efforts to engage it, and thus a key political impetus for Beijing to pursue this approach. Jilin is a landlocked province with a population of 27 million several million larger than the population of North Korea. Jilin has struggled to over come the legacy the role it shared with China's other Northeast provinces as a centerpiece of China's pre-reform planned industrial structure. Jilin's lack of coastal access has made this challenge more difficult. As the province has moved ahead with there structuring or closure many of its large-scale state-owned enterprises over the past two and a half decades, it has faced both unrest from laid off workers and difficulty attracting the foreign investment that has been an engine of growth for much of China, despite it relative proximity to two of China's most important sources of FDI, Japan and South Korea. With support from Beijing, Jilin has sought to over come its challenges by seeking to develop potential avenues to overcome these weaknesses. These have included seeking ways to integrate its own economy in the region, by reaching out not only to North Korea, but to Russia and the larger economies of Northeast Asia.[42]

Beijing's concerns about stability in Jilin and its Northeast

42. See Carla Freeman, China Reform Challenge: The Political Economy of Reform in China's Northeast, 1978-1998, (Johns Hopkins University PhD dissertation, 1998).

region also complicated by the presence of a substantial Korean minority population in Yanbian, the autonomous ethnic Korean prefecture that shares much of China's border with the DPRK. The "chaoxianzu ( )" have historically been important stakeholders in China's good relationship with North Korea as many continue to have relatives there, and they have been at the forefront of border trade with North Korea. More recently, as will be discussed, they have developed economic linkages to South Korea as well, which has raised Chinese concernsabout ethnic nationalism, including related sovereignty issues. China's significant central fiscal transfers to Yanbian aimed at boosting economic development there suggest an fort by Beijing to mitigate potential discontent within this population; however, while the result of these policies have been significant infrastructure and other improvements to China's side of the border, the region's development remains closely tied both to conditions under North Korea's control. So long as North Korea is perceived as a source of instability, international investment into the region will be limited; in addition, as long as North Korea fails to commit to open its economy to international trade, growth China's landlocked border region will be constrained.

Keeping the Border Open to Uncertain Engagement

For the first three decades of Kim Il Song's rule the North Korean economy expanded, its would-be autarky enabled by regular transfusions of support principally from the Soviet Union but also from China. Most cross-border exchanges between China and the DPRK then involved shipments of concessional goods by China to the North and assistance with labor, first in post-war reconstruction, and later in the construction of other engineering projects.[43]

43. Cheng Xiaohe states that as many as 1 million Chinese laborers worked in North Korea in the 1960s. Cheng Xiaohe, "The Evolution of Sino-North Korean Relations in the 1960s," Asian Perspective, (Vol. 34, No.2, 2010): 173-199, available at http://www.asianperspective.org/articles/v34n2-f.pdf.

Economic deprivation became a factor in the border dynamic between the two countries initially at the height of the Chinese Cultural Revolution, when it was Chinese citizens often ethnic Koreans, who crossed into North Korea seeking better conditions. As both political and economic circumstances within North Korea deteriorated, particularly after Kim's death in 1994, however, it has been North Koreans who have sought refuge in China, periodically in significant numbers. Most come across the border where it is divided by the narrow and shallow Tumen River into Jilin province. The ability of North Koreans to move across the Tumen into China may have contributed to reducing food deprivation within North Hamyong province during periods of famine.[44]

Initially, as others have documented, the Koreans who entered China illegally were frequently given assistance by Chinese Koreans, many of whom were reciprocating the help they had received from the North Korean side decades earlier. Local officials on the North Korean side of the border although aware that this was happening often looked the other way. Many of the DPRK citizens who crossed into Yanbian returned to North Korea, making regular crossings to obtain food and goods increasingly unavailable to them at home. As the flows increased, however, more refugees sought to stay on the Chinese side of the border and China began to crackdown on illegal migrants, returning them to North Korea according to a bilateral agreement between Beijing and Pyongyang.

Locals report that these harsher policies and the accompanying stigma attached to North Koreans who cross the border illegally, particularly since the Chinese

---

44. Stephen Haggard and Marcus Noland, Famine in North Korea: Markets, Aid, and Reform, (New York: Columbia University Press, 2007): 70.

government began its crackdown, along with the rising Han Chinese population in Yanbian, have reversed earlier attitudes of chaoxianzu toward North Korean "illegals." One Yanbian resident told one of the authors that although she felt that she and the North Koreans were "one ethnic group," in her view, trust was very low between people in Yanbian and those across the bridge in North Korea.[45] North Koreans are increasingly seen as a problem in the region associated with the smuggling and other illegal activity—a symptom of the country's brittle and dysfunctional economy, and a reminder of the ongoing uncertainty about its political stability as Kim Jung Il seeks to pass his political authority to his inexperienced son-- a foretaste of the humanitarian crisis that could spill across the border into Jilin and Liaoning.[46]

In this context, China's unprecedented leadership in the Six Party process can be seen as both aimed at the shared regional goal of North Korean denuclearization and regional peace and security, but also as one dimension of its effort to address the vulnerabilities to its borderland of North Korea's fragility. The security measures China also takes to mitigate this threat will be discussed later in this chapter. Ensuring that its border region not deprived of China's growth experience has thus become intertwined with China's North Korea policy. As the following will describe, as China has reached out to North Korea and has sought to interact with it economically, the local governments—from province to prefecture to the various cities—have been encouraged by Beijing to forgeties across the international border, playing a front line role in China's engagement with North Korea. Thus even as China has

45. Freeman, Interview, Yanbian (Tumen City) 2007.
46. Drew Thompson and Carla Freeman, " Flood Across the Border: China's Disaster Relief Operations and Potential. Response to a North Korean Refugee Crisis," US Korea Institute and The Nixon Center, (April 1, 2009); *see also*, ,http://www.dongcha.com/Article/ShowArticle.asp?ArticleID=6853

supported UN resolutions condemning North Korea's nuclear testing, economic exchanges between it and North Korea have continued to grow, facilitated by deliberate policies backed by generous funding, and to a certain extent enabled by the cultural and kinship ties of its chaoxianzu.

The largest trade volumes between China and North Korea flow across the border through Dandong, which is in direct line with North Korea's most industrialized region,including Pyongyang. Estimates suggest that as much as 70-75% of Chinese exports to North Korea pass through its port facilities. In recent years, even as North Korea move ahead with policies to further constrain free market activity in the country, it has taken steps that suggest a sustained interest in promoting trade at Dandong. In 2002, for example, it tried to attract investment to set up a special administrative region for trade and investment at its city of Sinuiju, linked by a "Friendship bridge" across the Yalu to Dandong. In 2009, a North Korean consular office was opened in Dandong. North Korea announced plans for new free trade areas on the Yalu River islands of Weihua Huangjinbing in early 2010. While in the early 2000s, North Korea looked to South Koreans as well as Chinese for investment in planned free trade zones, expectations now appear to be that it will be Chinese investment that provides the main negine for their development. Indeed, according to reports, Chinese companies have been given a 100 year lease to develop the two islands. China and North Korea have also agreed to construct a new bridge across the Yalu to enable greater traffic than the current Friendship Bridge can support.[47]

47. "China to Lease two DPRK Islands," North Korea Economy Watch, October 28, 2010, available at http://www.nkeconwatch.com/category/economic-reform/special-administrative-regions/sinuiju/; "MonthRecap: North Korea Brief," (No. 10-3-3-1, February 20, 2010), available at http:,//www.wilsoncenter.org/topics/pubs/100302_Monthly%20Recap%20(Feb%20 2010).pdf.

While Dandong is important in terms of sheer volume, nine of China's ten major border ports with North Korea are located in Jilin province, however. Key ports are in Yanbian Ethnic Korean autonomous prefecture. Yanbian shares a 233km border with Russia and 522km of Jilin's 1200km border with North Korea's Hamgyong-Bukdo province. It has an ethnic Korean population of about 830,000. Most of Yanbian's chaoxianzu trace their roots to northern Korean ancestors, who moved across the Tumen River after the Qing opened northeastern China to Korean emigration in the late 19th century, or their ancestors were forcibly relocated by Japan into Manchuria from Japan's then Korean colony as part of Japanese expansionism. Many did not receive formal Chinese citizenship until after the People's Republic of China (PRC) was established and some continue to maintain regular contacts with relatives across the border.[48]

While as a result of both Han in-migration and chaoxianzu out-migration, the chaoxianzu in Yanbian now represent only about 36% of the prefecture's total population, Yanji, the prefecture's capital, still has a Korean cultural feel. It is located at the heart of the Yanji plain, about 10km from the China-DPRK border. Most port facilities along Jilin's border with North Korea are imposing edifices that appear emblematic of China's dreams for the potential impact of expanded linkages between it and its neighbor. More open economic exchanges with North Korea would give Yanbian a convenient source of mineral and other resources as inputs for an expanding industrial base. In addition and importantly, with further infrastructure development,

48. Outi Luova, Ethnic Transnational capital. Transfers and Development-Utilization of Ties with South Korean in the Yanbian Korean Autonomous. Region, Autonomous Region, (Turku, Finland, Turun Yliopisto, 2007): 93. According to Luova, in the early 1990s, ethnic Koreans in Yanbian had 50,000 relatives in North Korea.

landlocked Yanbian would gain access to North Korean seaports.

The formal reopening of border trade between China and North Korea in 1982[49] was followed by the passage of a Regional Autonomy Law empowering Yanbian to undertake its own economic initiatives two years later.[50] But it was the easing of international tensions at the end of the Cold War first between China and Russia, and then between North and South Korea amid then President Roh's Nordpolitik, along with the normalization of China-South Korean relations, that put the spotlight on Yanbian as a potential new commercial hub for Northeast Asia. North Korea's promulgation in 1991of a joint venture law and the establishment of a Rajin-Sonbong ("Rason") Free Economic and Trade Area not far from the Chinese border had suggested that North Korea could be preparing to relax its strict commitment to its juche vision of economic self reliance.

Rason, a Chinese-style special economic zone (SEZ), was to have been among the hub of an ambitious UN-managed project, launched in 1992, to build a new international trading center, including a port city, centered on the Tumen River delta, where the borders of China, North Korea, and Russia meet that would have involved the post-modern step of pooling the sovereignty of the three countries. China, North Korea, South Korea, Mongolia, and later Russia cooperated in planning on the project with the UNDP and other technical experts. Some experts credit China with getting the UNDP

---

49. Li Dunqiu, "Economic and Social Implications of China-DPRK Border Trade for China's Northeast," National Bureau of Asian Research (2006), available at http.//www.nbr.org/downloads/pdfs/PSA/BS_Confo6_Li.pdf:4.
50. Luova (2007): 89

to undertake the scheme, which dovetailed with Jilin's own goals of obtaining coastal access.51 Jilin officials played a key role in convening a meeting on Northeast Asian cooperation held in Changchun in 1990 that set the stage for discussions among representatives of countries in the region and the UNDP.[52] Goals included integrating ports along the coast into transportation networks in the region, including the North Korean port of Rajin, into this trade and investment zone, so that cargo would be channeled from around Northeast Asia to different points in the region, and even westward to Europe via Mongolia. In addition to the development of regional logistics through this Tumen River Area Development Programme (TRADP), as it was then called, the idea was that it would also enable development based on the economic complementarities of the various participating countries, including natural resources,labor, and technology, creating an additional "growth pole" within Northeast Asia [53]

Scholar James Cotton has written extensively about the institutions in China involved in planning and implementation of the Tumen development scheme, including central, provincial and local bureaucratic participants organized within the "coordinating structures"

---

51. Gaye Christoffersen ""Nesting the Sino-Russian Border and the Tumen Project in the Asia-Pacific: Heilongjiang's Regional Relations," *Asian Perspective* (Vol. 20, No. 2, Fall winter 1996): 272.
52. James cotton,"China and Tumen River Cooperation: Jin's Coastal. Development Strategy," *Asian Survey, Vol. 36, No. 11 (November 1996): 1094.*
53. *Freeman, (1998) and Ian Davies, "Regional Cooperation in Northeast Asia – The Tumen River ArDevelopment Program, 1990–2000," North Pacific Policy Papers #4 (Vancouver: Institute of Asian Research, 2000): 31–37 (http://www.iar.ubc.ca/programs/PCAPS/pubs/nppp4.pdf).*

typical in China's policy making involving multiple layers of government or administrative entities. The importance of the project to the central government was reflected in the formation of a "Tumen River Area Leading Group" under the State Council and the State Science and Technology Committee, with involvement from other ministries and representation from the Jilin provincial government. Later, a provincial office for Tumen development was also established, with some provincial members serving on both the central and provincial body.[54] In addition to the visits to Yanbian by then Chinese President Jiang Zemin highlighting the opportunities represented by deepercooperation in the region, other important figures in the central government, such as Long Yongtu, Vice Minister of Foreign Trade and Economic Cooperation (MOFTEC), Long Yongtu, Vice Minister of Foreign Trade and Economic Cooperation (MOFTEC), known for his role negotiating China's accession to the World Trade Organization (WTO), were tapped by Beijing to join provinicial-Level leaders in representing China in meetings among the regional Tumen programme partcipants governing its progress.[55]

Peaceful Borders through Region-building

Although the original Tumen vision was abandoned for a range of reasons, including the very regional tensions it had hoped to ease and ultimately the Asian financial crisis, the program has endured, recast in the mid-2000s as the "Greater Tumen Initiative" (GTI). The GTI describes itself as

54. James Cotton, *Crossing Borders in the Asia Pacific: Essays on the Domestic-Foreign Policy Divide,* (New York : Nova Science Publishers, 2002):
55. Carla P. Freeman, "Neighborly Relations: the Tumen Development Project and China security strategy," Journal of Contemporary China, Vol. 19, No. 63, (2010): 145.
56. Greater Tumen Intitiative website, available at http:// www. tumenprogramme.org/

a "multilateral forum for the member countries to identify and implement regional initiatives that encourage economic growth, improve living standards and contribute to peace and stability in North-East Asia."[56] That the program lives on owes much to the tenacity of the UNDP. South Korea has continued to participate and Mongolia and Russia have stayed engaged, with local governments and think on tanks Japan's west coast also playing a role in keeping the programe alive. But it has been China's backing for Tumen regional development that has kept the project when it has been on the verge of collapse on critical life support. China has given the Tumen Secretariat a home in offices in Beijing since the program's operations were moved from UNDP headquarters in New York in 1994, and it appears that it was pressure (or encouragement) from China that kept North Korea involved in the project through periods of inter-Korean tensions, until recently.[57]

From Beijing's perspective, sustaining the Tumen project has served the objectives of its "good neighbor" policy to help build a stable regional environment for its own economic development even as it has underscored Beijing's commitment to regional cooperation. As it became clear, particularly following the death of Kim Il Sung, that a Korean Wiedervereinigung was not on the near horizon, the mechanism established to manage the Tumen project with its regular schedule of consultations among all participants China, Russia, and both North and South Korea, as well as Mongolia later, and Japan as an observer— also became valuable as a confidence building opportunity and a platform for dialogue about regional development issues among participating countries, including between the two Koreas, even as they continued to face off along the DMZ. Beijing has also recognized its importance to

57. Freeman, (2010).

the development of Jilin and Yanbian. As President Jiang Zemin declared in 1995, during one of a number of visits to the region, a knowledging the multi-tiered objectives of the scheme, "Develop Hunchun, develop the Tumen River, and develop cooperative relations with the countries of Northeast Asia."[58]

Yanbian, Jilin and South Korea

In the mid-1990s, Jilin's leadership called development of the Tumen region the most significant project in Jilin's opening to the outside world.[59] It recognized that the project could draw on the potential of its ethnic Korean minority to both attract investment from South Korea's booming economy into Jilin and Yanbian in particular, much as Guangdong had drawn investment from Hong Kong (and other overseas Chines), as well as to facilitate greatly expanded trade between China and North Korea. The story of South Korean investment in Jilin, and especially in Yanbian, however, offers a lesson in the challenges of building upon ethnic sympathies to foster economic linkages in China, given the hypersensitivity of Beijing to the potential for the politicization of ethnic identity. These sensitivities have ultimately contributed to reinforcing the importance of cross-border trade with North Korea in Yanbian and Jilin development policy.

---

58. Chan-Woo Lee, "Ten Years of Tumen River Area Development: Evaluation and Issues," ERINA Booklet, (Vol. 2, February 2003): 7.
59 Jean-Marc F. Blanchard, "Giving the Unrecognized their Due: Regional Actors, International Institutions, and Multilateral Economic Cooperation in Northeast Asia," in Daniel W. Dresner, (ed.), Locating the Proper Authorities: The Interaction of Domestic and International Institutions, (Ann Arbor: University of Michigan, 2003): 64; Sebastien Colin, 'A Border opening onto Numerous Geopolitical Issues," China Perspectives, 48 (2003), available at http://chinaperspectives.revues.org/385.

According to research by Finnish scholar, Outi Luova, initially, as opportunities are to expand links with South Korea, Yanbian officials, saw South Korean involvement in the local economy as politically unpalatable, even risky. Many with connections in North Korea were concerned about the impact of developing ties with South Korea on their relationship with their North Korean counterparts and also worried about the impact of such a move on the then modest but growing cross-border trade with North Korea.[60] However, others saw the potential connection of South Korea as vital to Yambian's economic future and used the possibility of attracting South Korean investment to enliven the local economy to lobby Beijing for an early extension of preferential policies to Yanbian's cities. Indeed, the Party-affiliated Yanbian Overseas Association (Yanbian haiwai lianyihui) itself sought to cultivate links to overseas Koreans investors.[61]

By the early 1990s, the push from province and prefecture combined with the momentum on the Tumen development project appeared to have yielded results: the central government made Hunchun, about 60km from the North Korean port of Rajin, an open border city and border economic cooperation zone and granted Yanji special "experimental reform" and development status.[62] The impact on local development was immediate: Hunchun, for example, saw a surge in foreign direct investment,

60. See Gao Xin, Lingdao Zhongguo de xinrenwu: Zhongguo shiliujie zhengzhiju dangwei:/ (China's New Top Leaders: Biography of the Members of China's 16th Politburo, (Vol 2).(Hong Kong: Mirror Books, 2003): 559.
61. Outi Luova, "Transnational Linkages and Development Initiatives in Ethnic Korean Yanbian Northest China: "Sweet and Sour" Capital Transfers, "*Pacific Affairs, (Vol. 82, No. 3 Fall 2009): 433.*
62. See discussion in Luova (2007): 90-95

with most of the 370 joint venture projects approved in the Hunchun Border Economic Cooperation Zone by 1994 coming from South Korea.

South Korean economic activity in Yanbian grew rapidly in the decade after PRC-ROK normalization, initially showing signs that it would outpace cross-border flows with North Korea. Within five years, 53% of all FDI in Yanbian was from South Korea, and two-way trade between the two sides was growing, with South Korea importing both raw materials and finished products (such as timber and timber products, but also textiles) from Yanbian and exporting equipment and processed goods back to the prefecture.[63]

Five years later by 2002, nearly three-quarters of all FDI in Yanbian came from South Korean sources.[64] South Korean investors were attracted to Yanbian not only by the Koreanspeaking labor, when they began investing in the prefecture, there was also a hope it would become a platform for expanded South Korean economic links to North Korea beyond the sensitive DPRK-ROK border.[65] By 2008,

63. Geoff Wright, " Trade and Investment Synergies in the Tumen Region," TREDA Advocacy Workshop *2002 Stiumulating Trade Investment and Growth In and Around the Tumen Region,* January 2000: 3; 22 available at http://www.tumenprogramme.org/data/upload/TREDA% 20 Advocacy% 20 Workshop, % Beijing, % 20 March% 202000/TRIS%20Paper%201pdf.
64. Luoua (2007): 124.
65. This had also been a motivation for investment as early as the 1980s by ethnic Koreans from the United States and other countries in Yanbian, especially those with family ties to the North: interview, Carla Freeman, Yanbian, December 2007. Through 2000, South Korean investment flowed principally to Northeast China, which accounted for above 85 percent of South Korean investment in China from 1993 to2000.[See Xiaohong Zhan, "Analysis of South Korea's Direct Investment in China," China & World Economy : 94-104, Vol. 13, No. 1, 2005: 100.]

however, South Korean investment reflected several years of a downward trend in Yanbian even as it was rising in China as a whole. Jilin data indicates that South Korean investment in the province fell from about 17% in 2001 of its total foreign investment to just over 7% in 2007.[66] Most South Korean investment in China was flowing to other regions. South Korean businessmen operating in Yanbian report that they feel South Korea's role in the prefecture's economy has proved politically sensitive, contributing to depressing South Korean investment there.[67] According to one source a concern that South Korean investors were treating Yanbian as a sort of "Korean territory" led some Chinese authorities to discourage South Koreans from providing "special assistance" to the region.[68]

Even so, while direct investment by South Korea in the prefecture has remained relatively modest,[69] South Korea has continued to factor significantly in Yanbian's economy through remittances. Exports of Korean-speaking labor from Yanbian to Korean-owned companies in South Korea and around the world represent a significant source of capital inflows to the prefecture -- as much as US $1 billion in a given

---

66. Lian Xiaomei, "An Analysis of the Current Status of the Introduction of Foreign Direct Investment in China's Jilin Province [in Japanese, Summary in English], (November 2009 Vol.90), available at http://www.erina.or.jp/en/Publications/er/pdf/Er90.pdf.
67. Authors' interviews, Beijing and Yanbian, December 2008.
68. C. H. Chai, Y. Y. Kueh, Clement Allan Tisdell (eds.), China and the Asia Pacific Economy, (New York, Nova Science Publishers, 1997): 215
69. Discussion Outi Luova, "Transnational Linkages and Development Initiatives in Ethnic Korean Yanbian, Northeast China: 'Sweet and Sour' Capital Transfers," Pacific Affairs, (Vol. 82, No. 3 Fall 2009): especially 441.

year.[70] Comparing visits to the region before these flows were occurring with more recent visits, the effect of this linkage has been to make Chinese Koreans more conscious of their distinct central identity. This is also suggested by the findings of some studies. One researcher has speculated that South Korea's international stature is among the factors that has contributed to a heightened sense of ethnic Korean pride. This amid intensifying irredentist rhetoric on the part of some South Koreans disputing China's sovereignty over Yanbian and other sections of territory along China's border with North Korea along with South Korea's plans to offer chaoxianzu South Korean citizenship, among other issues, all combined to intensify Beijing's concerns about South Korean interchanges with the prefecture.[71] And, these have also complicated how Beijing sees China's chaoxianzu, its "model minority," as it has been called, once known best in China for its contribution to China's revolutionary struggle. Punitive treatment (involving fines or even imprisonment) of those ethnic Korean Chinese who have taken South Korean citizenship and the prohibition of the use of the term 'overseas Korean' (chaoqiao) to refer to Chinese Koreans, offers evidence of growing concerns on the part of Chinese authorities about ethno-nationalism within its ethnic Korean population.[72] That a senior Chinese scholar of ethnic Korean descent appears to have provided South Korean officials with classified information has only intensified suspicions

70. Luova (2009): 427.
71. For discussion of this dispute see, for example, Yonson Ahn, "Competing Nationalisms: The mobilisation of history and archaeology in the Korea-China wars over Koguryo/Gaogouli," The Asia-Pacific Journal: Japan Focus, February 9, 2006, available at http://www.japanfocus.org/-Yonson-Ahn/1837.
72. Luova (2009): 442; Luova (2007): 28.

that ethnic Koreans could have dual loyalties.[73]

Chinese concerns about the impact of ethnic nationalism in the region are manifest in its "Northeast Project," a project of China's Center for the Study of Borderland History and Geography of the Chinese Academy of Social Sciences (CASS) with advisors from among China's senior leadership. According to a number of analyses, which look extensively at Chinese documents and commentary by researchers from CASS and China's Northeastern provinces participating in it, the project was launched in the early 2000s principally to counter potential irredentist claims by South Korea to Chinese territory, claims that could become more assertive in the event of North-South unification but in the meanwhile could be used to stir Korean nationalism among the chaoxianzu population.[74] The reaction to the project and other Chinese activities related to the history of the region, such as those conducted by Jilin's own Academy of Social Sciences,[75] by South Koreans has been strong, measurably affecting Korean perceptions of China and raising concerns on the part of some that China's long term strategic objective for the region is to recreate the ancient

---

73. "Renowned scholar Ji Xide arrested for 'spying for South Korea,"' Korea Times, (February 2, 2009), available at:http://www.koreatimes.co.kr/www/news/nation/2009/02/117_39943.html.
74. Yoon Hwy-tak, "China's Northeast Project: Defensive or Offensive Strategy?" East Asian Review, (Vol. 16, No. 4, Winter 2004): 99-121; Jae Ho Chung, "China's 'Soft Clash' with South Korea: The History War and Beyond," Asian Survey, (Vol. 49, Issue 3): 468–483.
75. Lee Yun-jeong, "Active Academic Exchanges: Northeast Asia's Future is Bright," Northeast Asian History Foundation News, available at: http://english.historyfoundation.or.kr/data/Newsletterlist/0906_eng/sub02.html.

Chinese order in which Korea functioned as a Chinese tributary. In September 2009, a group of 10 NGOs filed a petition with the International Court of Justice (ICJ) pursuing global recognition of territory essentially coterminous with Yanbian known as "Gando," part of the Korean territory.[76] If this ethnic consciousness or the threat thereof is indeed an emerging challenge among chaoxianzu, it is appearing at a time when other studies suggest that there is growing frustration by ethnic Koreans in China over a sense that their Korean cultural heritage constrains their opportunities for social advancement in China. One scholar's interviews with chaoxianzu concluded that ethnically Korean Chinese citizens see themselves "at the periphery of the Chinese economy." At the same time, however, they worry about the impact on their cultural identity of choosing to become educated in the Chinese language first rather than in Korean in order to compete more effectively in the mainstream.[77] Anecdotal data suggests that ethnically Korean Chinese value the preferential policies extended to them by virtue of their minority status, including their exemption from the one-child policy and the special fiscal transfers that ethnic autonomous regions receive, and are worried about

---

76. "Korean Group File Claim over Lost Korean Territory," ROK Drop, September 9, 2009, available at: http://rokdrop.com/2009/09/09/korean-group-files-claim-with-icj-over-lost-gando-territory/.
77. Fang Gao, "What it Means to be a 'Model Minority': Voices of Ethnic Koreans in Northeast China," Asian Ethnicity, Vol. 9, No. 1, February 2008: 63; also in Si Joong Kim, "The Economic Status and Role of Ethnic Koreans in China," Institute for International Economics: 119, available at www.iie.com/publications/chapters_preview/365/6iie3586.pdf.

losing these entitlements.[78] Rumors, fed by the South Korean blogosphere, also circulate that because of the declining share of Koreans in the prefecture, it may lose its autonomous status.[79]

Fiscal Flows: Prosperous Borders, Western Development, and Revitalize the Northeast

Concerns about South Korean-led ethnic nationalism along its longest border with the Korean peninsula may have helped put a chill on direct South Korean economic activity in the prefecture but has only helped opened the sluices wider for extraordinary fiscal flows into Yanbian. Since it was established in 1952, Yanbian's autonomous status has made it the beneficiary of special policies for minority regions in China, including fiscal transfers for fixed asset development from central funding sources.[80] In recent decades, Yanbian's border counties have received significant funding from the PBWM program, which is aimed directly at poverty alleviation projects in rural chaoxianzu communities, ranging from various small-scale agricultural development projects to clean water supply development to tourism to developing programs to connect

78. Authors' visits to the region, especially December 2007 (Freeman) and December 2008 (Freeman and Thompson); see also "Close ties between Han Chinese, ethnic Koreans in China's Jilin Province," September 5. 2009 available at http://www.channelnewsasia.com/stories/eastasia/view/1002916/1/.html.
79. Informal discussions by the authors, Yanbian 2008 and Beijing 2010.
80. "Governor Han Changfu Accepts Interview from China Radio International (CRI) Chinese and Foreign Reporters," July 23, 2009, available at http://english.jl.gov.cn/jilin/200907/t20090723_608733.html; , , , available at: http://www.cpirc.org.cn/yjwx/yjwx_detail.asp?id=27.

rural laborers to urban and even international demand for labor,[81] Progress has been measured by the increase in rural incomes in ethnic Korean villages, and by the number of small businesses started by former rural residents who have emigrated to urban areas. According to one analysis of the PBWM's impact on the ethnic Korean population in China, the rate of rural to urban migration by the Korean population in Yanbian and in Northeast China more generally has exceeded the rate for Han Chinese.[82]

In addition, although far from western China, Yanbian has also received WDP funding, much directed toward the construction of transportation infrastructure. Between 2001 and 2006, Yanbian received fiscal transfers totaling more than 19 billion RMB, representing about a quarter of all central WDP-related transfers to Jilin for its minority regions. This funding has been used for highway and rail expansion as well as for so-called "social development" (health and education) projects. In addition to WDP funding, Yanbian has also received central funding from the program to "Revitalize the Northeast," introduced in the late 1990s to help China's Northeast region reform its heavily industrialized region, at a time when restructuring of large state-owned industries was threatening labor unrest. Yanbian boasts that it is the only region in China to receive funding from all three major central programs: the PBWM, WDP, and RNE.[83]

---

81. "" : , (July 19, 2010) available at: http://cn.iybtv.com/Html/ybyw/20100719/683932455.html;2010-11-22 http://big5.cri.cn/gate/big5/city.cri.cn/29344/2010/11/22/3866s2546539.htm
82. (3) (January 7, 2010), available at: http://www.lunwenbiye.com/jiaoyulei/20100107179_3.html.
83. Freeman, Interview Yanbian Bureau of Commerce, December 2007.

Along with the new network of highways connecting Jilin and its border region more deeply to the rest of China, substantial public investment has also gonc to develop the infrastructure for regional trade, including linking Yanbian to the broader region along the lines proposed by the original Tumen development scheme.[84]The orientation of these efforts has been toward North Korea. The impressive border port facilities found along China's border with North Korea such as the facilities at Hunchun and Quanhe, for example, were expanded in 1999-2000 to handle a capacity of 600,000MT each. According to one estimate, RMB500 million had been spent on border port renovation to upgrade Yanbian's border crossings with the DPRK.[85] Much of this investment is linked to expanding the province's access to Rajin, North Korea's ice-free port—developed by Japan in the 1930s,[86] as part of what Jilin provincial officials desperate for coastal access have called "connecting [to] the sea by borrowing ports."[87] In 2008, with investment through

---

84. 2001-2006 [Yanbian Western Development Report 2001-2006] Yanbian Development and Reform Commission, available at http://www.ybxx.gov.cn/jjqk_xxnc/7/01.html.
85. "Port Development in Jilin Province,"Yanbian Commodities website, January 3, 2011, available at http://www.zhenhuaexpo.com/en_news_show.asp?infoid=235.
http://www.zhenhuaexpo.com/en_news_show.asp?infoid=235.
86. Evelyn McCune and Shannon McCune," The Tumen River Corridor," Far Eastern Survey, Vol. 14, No. 12 (Jun. 20, 1945): 166.
87. Presentation to the Tumen Secretariat, Wang Xiaoping, "Promote the development and opening-up of Changjitu Pilot Area," April 19, 2010, available at www.tumenprogramme.org/.../PresentationbyMr.WangXiaoping,Jilin_eng_GfkQzn.doc

Hunchun in conjunction with the Economic Cooperation Bureau of the Rason People's Commission in North Korea, a Sino-DPRK joint venture called Rason International Logistics was registered in Rason with the purpose of expanding port facilities and developing an industrial park in the vicinity of Rajin.

Promoting Cross-border Trade

These investments went hand in hand with the designation by North Korea of Rason as a free trade zone" and a "special development city." The goal for China is to develop a highway between Quanhe and Rajin that will be monitored but will effectively allow the free flow of goods -coal, iron ore, and other minerals, as well as some food products from North Korea and processed goods and equipment from China-- across the border.[88] Investment in Rajin port expansion has proceeded in fits and starts, spurred by a visit by Kim Jong Il to Rason in early 2010. In 2008 North Korea has granted a 50-year lease of one pier to Russia and extended a 10-year lease on another pier to a Chinese company a year later.[89] At the time of writing, rumors on China's commitment to developing the Rajin port abound. Some reports suggest that Jilin province

88. Wang Jun, "Freeing up Transport in Northeast Asia," March 10, 2008, available at http://www.tumenprogramme.org/news.php?id=520; Gao Xinli, "Border Trade North Korea's Economic Lifeline," Global Times, July 26 2010, available at http://opinion.globaltimes.cn/commentary/2010-07/556087.html.
89. Scott Snyder, "North Korea's Renewed Push for Foreign Investment at Rajin-Sonbong," available at http://www.eastasiaforum.org/2010/03/12/north-koreas-renewed-push-for-foreign-investment-at-rajin-sonbong/

alone earmarked as much as RMB3 billion for Rajin port development.[90] Another report indicated that late in 2010, China's Commerce Ministry signed an agreement with North Korea to develop the port, committing USD3.5 billion over five years beginning in 2011.[91]

Beijing's efforts to persuade North Korea to open its economy have been met with mixed signals from Pyongyang. On the one hand the Dear Leader has repeatedly reassured Chinese leaders that he is committed to a "government-led market operation"[92] and gave his personal benediction to restarting the dormant free-trade zone in Rason. Pyongyang has also given a green light to the development of additional open economic zones in the Yalu near Dandong. On the other hand North Korea has tightened restrictions on exports and closed its border to external trade in times of crisis. When after its second nuclear test of May 2009, China sharply criticized North Korea and cast its vote in support of UNSC resolution 1874,[93] Pyongyang withdrew from the Greater Tumen Initiative, a move consistent with similar moves, such as its border closure following China's normalization of relations with South Korea, during its first nuclear test in 2006, and again in late 2008 amid rumors that Kim Jong Il had suffered a stroke.

---

90. Institute for Far Eastern Studies, "DPRK-PRC Summit and the Outlook for Bilateral Economic Cooperation," May 11, 2010: http://ifes.kyungnam.ac.kr/eng/m05/s10/content.asp?nkbriefNO=362&GoP=1
91. "Rumored $3.5b Chinese Investment Deal," North Korea Economy Watch, December 30, 2010, available at http://www.nkeconwatch.com/category/economic-reform/foreign-direct-investment/.
92. Kim Chul (,), "," KDI North Korea Economic Review, Issue 10, No.
93. Bonnie Glaser, "China's Policy in the Wake of the Second DPRK Nuclear Test," China Security (Vol. 5 No. 2, 2009): 3, available at http://asiafoundation.org/resources/pdfs/GlaserChinaSecurity2.pdf.

Certainly, the deprivation associated with this self imposed suspension of trade is borne principally by the North Korean side, but the impact of North Korean limits on trade is hard-felt in some parts of the Chinese side of the border, which rely on cross-border trade, as well. Uncertainty about North Korean actions has bred a sense of frustration and disappointment in Yanbian. One official in the Yanbian foreign commercial office bemoaned the lack of opportunities for his child in the region and the impact that that has on families in the region, as he expected that his daughter would have to move to other parts of China for work. He noted that his family was already divided. He still had relatives in North Korea, including his father's sisters, and was disappointed that North Korea had failed to open its economy, which he felt would create many new opportunities in Yanbian.[94] A court clerk interviewed by one of the authors in Tumen reported that processing divorces was her principal activity as couples separated in order to leave the region -with many women hoping to find new mates in South Korea.[95] (Ironically, reports suggest that this pattern has led to a greater demand among ethnic Korean men in the prefecture who cannot find mates among their compatriots for North Korean wives—a demand that can have a dark side when these wives are obtained through human traffickers.)[96] Businessmen lament the prohibitive costs of uncertainty, and a recent piece in the English language *China Daily* described the port of Tumen as a "silent city," noting that about 80 percent of its ethnic Korean population now works in South Korea due to the poor

94. Freeman, interview Yanbian 2007.
95. Freeman interviews, Yanbian (Tumen), 2007.
96. Ming Liu, "China and the North Korean Crisis: Facing Test and Transition,"
Pacific Affairs, Vol. 76, No. 3 (Fall, 2003): 353.

business climate. [97] The article connected Tumen's failure to thrive to North Korea's restrictive trade policies in contrast with Jilin's efforts to engage in commerce with its neighbor. In 2008 Jilin changed its regulations to provisionally allow the settlement of border trade with North Korea in RMB and permitting North Korean banks and individuals to set up RMB accounts to facilitate border trade.[98] A market to sell North Korean products in Tumen was launched in the fall of 2010, but while transactions below RMB8,000 are tax exempt, erratic participation in and restrictions on trade within North Korea have meant that the market's stalls have mainly stood empty. This recalls a similar experiment with cross-border trade at Quanhe, where after two years of lively trading activity, a sudden shift in North Korean policy to restrict the outflow of foreign currency brought trade flows to a halt.[99] One Chinese scholar (an ethnic Korean) at Yanbian University has declared the region a "dead border" as a result of North Korea's ambivalence about opening its economy,[100] and move like its currency reform and other efforts to aimed at eradicating the market networks that have arisen amid the failures of the planned

97. "Dead Border' Is Price of China Support for North Korea Regime," Bloomberg.com, June 14, 2010, available at http://www.businessweek.com/news/2010-06-14/-dead-border-is-price-of-china-support-for-north-korea-regime.html; "Silent City," China Daily, November 19, 2010: 18, available at http://www.china-daily.org/China-News/13-cities-in-Liaoning-Dandong-Yalu-River-brewing-co-creating-economic-zone/.
98. Kim Chul (), "," KDI North Korea Economic Review, Issue 10, No. 5 May 2008: , 56-72,, available at www.nktech.net/data/research/kc200805017.pdf.
99. Li (2006):9
100. "Silent City," China Daily, November 19, 2010: 18

distribution system.[101]

Nonetheless, while some Chinese scholars have expressed skepticism that the zones will move forward, Beijing has persisted in trying to find ways to encourage North Korea to engage in cross-border trade and investment, moving ahead with its own infrastructure development aimed in part at facilitating cross-border economic linkages. North Korea may have withdrawn from the Greater Tumen Initiative (GTI) but China has persisted with its own Tumen development plans, which continue to involve and indeed be directed toward engaging North Korea. A project referred to as " China's Tumen River Area Development Plan" with Jilin as its centerpiece received State Council approval in August 2009. The plan links Yanbian to Changchun (through an infrastructure development scheme known as Changchun, Jilin -Tumen or " Chang-Ji-Tu") with parts of Liaoning province, Heilongjiang province and Inner Mongolia, encompassing regions that have been focal points of the Greater Tumen Initiative. According to the director of Tumen River Development Division of the Bureau of Economic & Technological Cooperation for Jilin Province, the Chang-Ji-Tu plan aims to "to further enhance the level of opening up along the border;" support the "process of the further implementation of the revitalization of northeast old industrial base;" and "[create] new mechanisms for international cooperation and building platforms for international communication is an important

101. Bradley O'Babson, "Reform or Retrenchment:An Economist's Perspective on Recent Events in North Korea," February 23, 2010, 38 North, available at http://38north.org/2010/03/reform-or-retrenchment-an-economist%e2%80%99s-perspective-on-recent-events-in-north-korea-by-bradley-o-babson/.

measure to enhance Tumen River international cooperation mechanism..."[102] Its role in China's ongoing efforts to encourage North Korea to open its economy and deepen cooperation with China was made apparent when Chinese Premier Wen Jiabao specifically introduced the plan during his visit to North Korea in October 2009, only months after North Korea withdrew from the GTI.[103] Jilin's Vice Governor Chen Weigen subsequently traveled to Pyongyang to provide details on planning for the scheme.[104]

China Inc. in North Korea?

As a result, as North Korea's international isolation has grown, its relative economic relationship with China has also grown disproportionately, with reports estimating that China accounted for about 53 percent of the North's cross-border trade in 2009.[105] Chinese exports to North Korea have expanded steadily, outpacing Chinese imports of North Korean minerals and other products, so that in 2009, the value of China's exports to North Korea were more than two and a half times the value of North Korea's imports,

102. Presentation to the Tumen Secretariat, Wang Xiaoping, "Promote the development and opening-up of Changjitu Pilot Area," April 19, 2010, available at www.tumenprogramme.org/.../PresentationbyMr.WangXiaoping,Jilin_eng_GfkQzn.doc
103. Institute for Far Eastern Studies, "DPRK-PRC Summit and the Outlook for Bilateral Economic Cooperation," May 11, 2010: http://ifes.kyungnam.ac.kr/eng/m05/s10/content.asp?nkbriefNO=362&GoP=1
104. " N. Korea and China to Jointly Develop Two N. Korean Cities," The Hankyoreh, June 17, 2010, available at http://english.hani.co.kr/arti/english_edition/e_national/426105.html.
105. " North Korean Economic Reliance on China Further Growing: Report," Yonhap News Agency, October 7, 2010, available at http://english.yonhapnews.co.kr/n_northkorea/2010/10/06/28/4301000000AEN20101006005600325F.HTML

leaving a trade deficit of over USD1 billion.[106] Some experts calculate that around 90 percent of North Korea's energy imports and 45 percent of North Korea's food come from China.[107] The Chinese renminbi now circulates within North Korea, with one Chinese expert calculating that renminbi in circulation in North Korea in 2004 had already reached an estimated RMB2.75 billion, up from only RMB300 million in 2001, an increase of 900%.[108] North Korean entities have settled trade in RMB through banks in China's border areas for some time, with nearly 80% of settlement carried out in RMB by 2006.[109] One of the reasons Jilin suffers when North Korea chooses to close it own borders is that North Korea is now Jilin's fourth largest trading partner.[110]

106.Eurostat data, available at http://trade.ec.europa.eu/doclib/docs/2006/september/tradoc_113366.pdf.107. Jayshree Bajoria, "The China-North Korea Relationship, "Council on Foreign Relations, October 7, 2010, available at http://www.cfr.org/publication/11097/chinanorth_korea_relationship.html.

107.Jayshree Bajoria, "The China-North Korea Relationship, "Council on Foreign Relations, October 7, 2010, available at http://www.cfr.org/publication/11097/chinanorth_korea_relationship.html.

108. Citing data from reports by Wang Liyuan in 2005 and Tao Shigui of Nanjing Normal University in 2006, Reginald Smith, "China's 'little dollar' spreads its wings," Asia Times on-line, January 28, 2010, available at http://www.atimes.com/atimes/China_Business/LA28Cb01.html.

109."The Use of The Renminbi for Trade and Non-Trade Denomination," China Economist Magazine, March 2, 2010 available at http://www.globaltrade.net/international-trade-import-exports/f/market-research/pdf/China/Banking-Finance-and-Insurance-The-Use-Of-The-Renminbi-For-Trade-And-Non-Trade-Denomination.html.

110.Jilin Provincial Government, Foreign Affairs Office, en.changchun.gov.cn/e/content.aspx%3FID%3D1038%26url%3Dxw/content+Choe+Yung-rim+Jilin&cd=10&hl=en&ct=clnk&gl=us

China's direct investments in North Korea have also expanded. From the mid-2000s, as China's foreign reserves started to accumulate and it launched its "going out strategy" to encourage its firms to invest directly overseas, Chinese companies started exploring investment opportunities in North Korea. In 2003, China's official statistics report that reported outward FDI to the DPRK stood at a modest USD 1.12 million; the same figures indicate that it had increased to USD 41.23 million by 2008, numbers useful principally in so far as they suggest the dramatic increase in investment as this is far below the level of commitments and actual investments that have been made.[111] Reports suggest that the value of committed investments by Chinese firms could be many fold greater. [112]

Although some deals are more clearly linked than others to political objectives, others also have clear economic objectives for Beijing. For example, Beijing took steps to assist its firms in entering the North Korean market by negotiating an "Investment Encouragement and Protection Agreement" with Pyongyang in 2005 and through such policy measures as treating exports from North Korea that were processed in Rajin using Chinese materials as domestic products, thereby exempting them from customs procedures.[113] China has also pursued and won exclusive mining and fishery rights in North Korea in exchange for upfront payment

---

111.rim+Jilin&cd=10&hl=en&ct=clnk&gl=us
52 2008 Statistical Bulletin of China's
Outward Foreign Direct Investment, availableat
http://hzs2.mofcom.gov.cn/aarticle/
statistic/200909/20090906535723.htm

112.Jae Cheol Kim, "The Political Economy of Chinese Investment in North Korea: A Preliminary Assessment," Asian Survey, Vol. 46, Issue 6 (2006):907.

113. Kim (2006): 908.

for access to these resources.[114] By 2009, China reportedly had 20 investment projects involving minerals extraction in North Korea. Other significant investments since 2004 have included China National Offshore Oil Corporation's deal on Yellow Sea offshore exploration rights.[115]

China's Dealmakers

Who or what actually is "China" in these deals? In many sectors, "China" means firms from Jilin. It was Jilin's state-owned Tonghua Iron and Steel Group that was given access (in exchange for substantial investment) for a 50 year period to North Korea's Musan mine, about 10 kilometers from the China-North Korean border.[116] The deal was one of a package of deals negotiated by the Jilin provincial government that would involve Jilin providing power

114. John S. Park, "North Korea, Inc.: Gaining Insights into North Korean Regime Stability from Recent Commercial Activities," US Institute of Peace Working Paper, April 22, 2009: 9, available at http://www.nkeconwatch.com/nk-uploads/north-korea-inc.pdf.
115. Kim, Sang Hun, "Current Situations on Sino-North Korea Economic Cooperation (Korean)" KDI North Korea Economy Review, Aug. 31, 2010, available at http://210.114.108.30/kdi/report/report_read04.jsp?1=1&pub_no=11523.51.
116. "Pramod Mittal Eyes Stake in DPRK Mines," North Korea Economy Watch, April 4, 2010, available at: http://www.nkeconwatch.com/category/dprk-organizations/state-offices/musan-mine/; US Department of the Interior and US Geological Survey, Minerals Yearbook, Volume III: Area Reports: International 2005, Asia and the Pacific, (Washington DC, US Government Printing Office, 2007): 15-2. Pyongyang reportedly terminated the agreement with Tonghua in 2010.

to North Korea in exchange for access to minerals.[117] It was two Hunchun city companies that negotiated an agreement with authorities to use some port facilities in Rajin for 50 years, and although it was a Dalian (Liaoning) company that signed the deal to lease a berth at the port, the deal was announced by the Party secretary of Yanbian prefecture, Li Longxi,[118] (In January 2011, Jilin newspapers celebrated the arrival of the first shipment of provincial coal to Shanghai via the port of Rajin, by a Hunchun shipping company.[119]) By the end of 2006, according to one source, more than two-dozen enterprises from Jilin had won approval from China to invest in North Korea, bringing the total value of Jilin's investment to an estimated 38% of China's total accumulated FDI in North Korea since 2000.[120] Yanbian's party secretary also reported that as many as 20 companies from Yanbian alone, involved in everything from cigarette and pharmaceutical production to aquaculture and mining, have invested nearly USD 70 million in North Korea.[121]

117."China Expanding Steel Industry in North Korea," Resource Investor, November 1, 2005, available at http://www.resourceinvestor.com/News/2005/11/Pages/China-Expanding-Steel-Industry-in-North-Korea.aspx.

118.(2010-03-3116:07:42)http://blog.sina.com.cn/s/blog_4f0f6add0100honl.html

119." hexun.com, (January 20,2011), available at http://news.hexun.com/2011-01-20/126914096.html.

120.http://www.investment.jl.cn/article.jsp?id=4880

121. 6823, March 25, 2010, http://blog.sina.com.cn/s/blog_4f0f6add0100honl.html; another source suggests that by 2010, Jilin had invested USD110 million in North Korea across 35 projects, see Jilin Provincial Government, Foreign Affairs Office. en.changchun.gov.cn/e/content.aspx%3FID%3D1038%26url%3Dxw/content+Choe+Yung-rim+Jilin&cd=10&hl=en&ct=clnk&gl=us.

Data from variety of sources confirms the trend of a steady increase in Chinese FDI to North Korea, in which outflows from Jilin sources consistently represent a significant share.

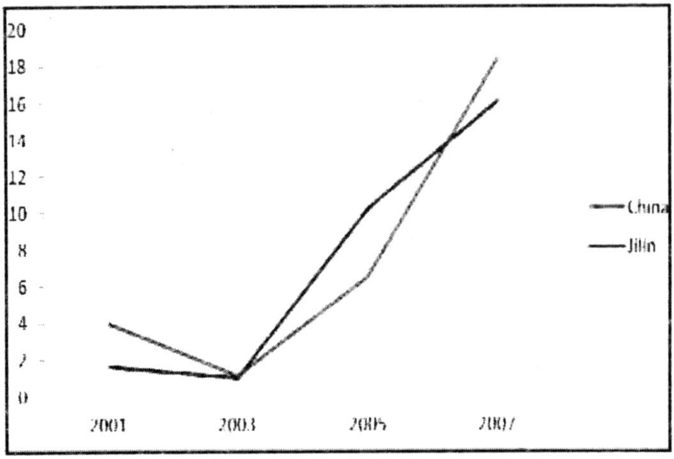

China and Jilin, actual committed/year to North Korea USD million (various sources)[122]

Local leaders from both sides of the border are direct facilitators of these deals. The recently concluded deal between China and North Korea to construct hydroelectric generating stations on the Yalu involved municipal Party Committee leaders from various border cities, who hosted members of the DPRK's National Electric Power Industry, for example. Other Jilin cities and counties have also concluded deals with counterparts in nearby border regions

---

122.Wu Hao,"The Current Status of and Prospects for the Economic Relations between China's Jilin Province and the DPRK,"[in Japanese] Erina Report, Vol. 88, July 2009): 8; 2008 Statistical Bulletin of China's Outward Foreign Direct Investment, available at: ttp://hzs2.mofcom.gov.cn/aarticle/statistic/200909/20090906535723.htm Liu Ming, "China's Role in the Course of North Korea Transition," available at http://www.nautilus.org/publications/essays/napsnet/reports/Liu.pdf;http://www.360doc.com/content/07/0413/16/7579_445554.shtml; ", April 14, 2007.

in North Korea to develop mines.[123]

Larger-scale deals involving provincial-level state owned enterprises are formally concluded on the Chinese side with support from the provincial government, often at the vice-governor level. Investment and trade promotion initiatives that are focused on one province or region also involve the participation of both central and local leaders. The provincial Foreign Affairs Office plays a key role in organizing logistics and providing support to visiting dignitaries.[124]

High level North Korean officials have been regular visitors to Northeast China. In 2010 alone, first Kim Jong Il held unofficial talks with Chinese President Hu Jintao in Changchun, Jilin's capital, where he notably recalled his time living in Jilin and indicated, according to an official Chinese foreign ministry report, that "he was touched... to see its great changes and development..."[125] His visit was followed by a visit of a large delegation comprising senior central and provincial Chinese leaders among them Zhou Yongkang, member of the Standing Committee of the Political Bureau of the Central Committee and secretary of the Central Commission of Politics and Law of the Communist Party of China, Wang Jiarui, head of the International Liaison

123."," Journal of Yanbian University, (June 2009), Vol 1.42, No.3: 45

124. "Foreign Affairs and Overseas Chinese Affairs Meeting of Jilin Province Held in Changchun," jl.gov.cn, February 16, 2009, available at http://wb.jl.gov.cn/english/NewsinBrief/200902/t20090216_523554.htm.
February 16, 2009, available at http://wb.jl.gov.cn/english/NewsinBrief/200902/t20090216_523554.htm.

125.Hu Jintao Holds Talks with Kim Jong Il in Changchun," PRC, Ministry of Foreign Affairs, (August 20, 2010), available at http://www.fmprc.gov.cn/eng/zxxx/t736661.htm.

Department of the C.C., the CPC, Sun Zhengcai, secretary of the Jilin Provincial Committee of the CPC, Zhang Zhijun, vice-minister of Foreign Affairs, Chen Jian, vice-minister of Commerce, Chen Xi, deputy secretary of the Liaoning Provincial Committee of the CPC, and Du Yuxin, deputy secretary of the Heilongjiang Provincial Committee, as well as Liu Hongcai, Chinese ambassador to the DPRK. The delegation was hosted by its counterparts within North Korea, including senior North Korean leaders, and the chief secretaries of relevant North Korean provinces.[126]

This visit was reciprocated by a delegation of a dozen North Korean mayoral and provincial chiefs, who toured food, chemical plants and agricultural facilities.[127] Subsequently, North Korea's premier also traveled to Jilin as well as Heilongjiang and Liaoning province with a delegation of around 30 officials, including many technocrats. In Jilin, Choe Yung-rim was greeted by Zhang Dejiang, China's Korean-speaking vice-premier who graduated from Kim Il Sung university and later served in the Yanbian leadership. Choe and his delegation visited factories, including Jilin First Autoworks, and was briefed on the "Chang-Ji-Tu" project by Jilin governor Wang Rulin in meetings attended by all high ranking provincial officials, including the Party Secretary, and Ambassador Liu Hongcai.[128] These exchanges of delegations accord with

---

126 "Reception Given for Chinese Party Delegation," KCNA, October 9, 2010, available at http://www.kcna.co.jp/item/2010/201010/news09/20101009-32ee.html.

127 "Rumored $3.5b Chinese Investment Deal," North Korea Economy Watch, December 30, 2010, available at http://www.nkeconwatch.com/category/economic-reform/foreign-direct-investment/.

128.Jilin Provincial Government, Foreign Affairs Office.en.changchun.gov.cn/e/content.aspx%3FID%3D1038%26url%3Dxw/content+Choe+Yung-rim+Jilin&cd=10&hl=en&ct=clnk&gl=us

the formula prescribed during Hu's meeting with Kim that "China is ready to develop trade and economic cooperation in the principles of government guidance with enterprises playing a major role, market operation, and mutual benefits for win-win results."[129]

Managing Cross-border Security

Even as China has continued to prop up North Korea's economy by seeking to provide an enabling environment for bilateral trade and investment flows into North Korea by its companies, it has also hedged against the potential spillover effects from the increasingly desperate conditions within North Korea by increased security along its side of the border. In 2003, China moved PLA border defense forces to both its North Korean and Myanmar borders. While some experts have suggested that this move was part of a broader force restructuring process and a response to corruption among the People's Armed Police, it is also reasonable to speculate that these PLA troops were moved in anticipation of a crisis, humanitarian or security, on the Korean peninsula.[130] Rumors abound about the development of a special Chinese force to deal with a significant crisis along the North Korean border, including the creation of a

---

129.Chinese Foreign Ministry, "Hu Jintao Holds Talks with Kim Jong Il in Changchun , August 30, 2010: http://www.fmprc.gov.cn/eng/zxxx/t736661.htm.

130.Chinese experts have asserted that this restructuring related an interest in bringing all borders into conformity and that the substitution of the PLA for the Ministry of Public Security which had had responsibility for external security in these areas since 1981 had nothing to do with the nuclear crisis on the Korean peninsula, see M. Taylor Fravel, "Securing Borders: China's Doctrine and Force Structure for Frontier Defense," The Journal of Strategic Studies, Volume 30.4-5 (August-October 2007): 728.

force composed only of ethnic Korean Chinese troops.[131]

Management of both the emergency response system as well as day-to-day and so-called non-traditional border security falls to Jilin province, which also coordinates directly with its North Korean counterparts. The joint protocol on border security between China and North Korea provides for regular contact between the two sides' security forces, including routine representative meetings every few years by border security leadership and provides for possible cooperation on disaster management and other security work in the border region.[132]

It is the local border police who must contend with the rising number of North Koreans who enter the province illegally and with increased cross-border crime, from smuggling to drug and human-trafficking. A recent report identified Yanbian as well as Changbai Korean Autonomous County in Jilin, along with Dandong as key conduits for North Korean drugs—mainly methamphetamines—into China.[133] Reports suggest that drug trafficking is a growing

131.Joshua Stanton, "China Prepares North Korea Occupation Force," Open Radio, September 10, 2009, available at http://www.freekorea.us/2009/09/10/open-radio-china-prepares-n-korea-occupation-force/

132.Interview Chinese scholar, 2009. A s along other borders, border residents wishing to visit relatives across the border may be issued a border pass, although relatives designated "non-immediate" family must go through a special application process. Border work passes may also be provided to civil servants whose work frequently takes them across the border. "," www changbai. gov. cn, available at http://cb.cbs.gov.cn/BsWebCms/site/cbxcms/news/n2717977190.html

133.Yong-an Zhang, "Drug Trafficking from North Korea: Implications for Chinese Policy," Brookings, December 3, 2010, available at http://www.brookings.edu/articles/2010/1203_china_drug_trafficking_zhang.asp.

problem in Jilin.[134] The shooting by North Korean border guards of three Chinese civilians in June 2010 near Dandong in Liaoning was given unusual publicity by the Chinese government, but there is evidence that along some parts of the border, it is not unusual for rogue North Korean soldiers to cross into China and engage in robbery and other criminal activity. Other reports suggest that North Korean forces have crossed into China to detain (and even kill, as was reported in early 2011) defectors. While there is no obvious physical evidence of this as one travels along the border, Jilin has tightened not only electronic surveillance, including the use of GIS,[135] it has intensified patrols along the border, a move, according to some reports, matched by additional North Korean patrols in some border areas. The level and quantity of technology deployed by the Yanbian Military Sub-district has jumped significantly in recent years, with the use of border sensors and video providing 24-hour monitoring and control.[136] Emergency management pertaining to border control has also been strengthened through the linkage of designated households to border police and a new emphasis on training for early response.[137]

---

134. "More Foreigners Involved in Drug Trafficking Cases," China Daily, June 26, 2010, available at http://english.cri.cn/6909/2010/06/26/189s579348.htm.
135. "GIS Applications in the Security Border Management," State Bureau of Surveying and Mapping, October 15, 2007, available at http://www.sbsm.gov.cn/article//chcg/cgyy/200812/20081200046140.shtml
136. LeeSungJin,"10,000MoreTroopsforYangkang,"September 14, 2009, Daily NK, available at http://www.dailynk.com/english/read.php?cataId=nk01500&num=5402
137., "--" [National Public Emergency Management Mechanisms,JilinProvince,YanbianAutonomousPrefecture's Hunchun as an Example] (2009) http://cpfd.cnki.com.cn/Article/CPFDTOTAL-XZGL201002001027.htm.

Mobile police units in vehicles equipped with sophisticated communications equipment are among the high-tech investments made by Jilin to improve security along its border with North Korea.[138]

Along with these security measures, Jilin maintains a fairly well-developed civilian emergency response system that could be mobilized in the event of a flood of refugees from North Korea and would coordinate with the PLA to manage such a crisis.[139]

Implications for US Policy

China's border region with North Korea has played a critical part in the drama of China's efforts to use economic inducements, including infrastructure linkages, natural resources development and energy joint-ventures, to try to persuade its neighbor that it has a stake in regional stability. Constrained by its commitment to the principle of "noninterference," China is trying to reshape North Korea through a "constructive engagement" approach. Jilin is an immediate stakeholder in this approach, as the decisions that Pyongyang makes about its own economic and security policy weigh heavily in its economic success or failure. Jilin provincial and other local leaders are important actors in China's interactions with North Korea, as are Jilin companies, many with extensive experience in North Korea or even ethnic ties to the peninsula.

However, China's cross-border engagement with North Korea is aimed at relatively narrow interests: preventing

---

138.World News Connection, PRC Yanbian Military Sub District Informatizes border Patrols, Jiefangjun Bao Online (October 6, 2009); World News Connection,"Report on DPRK-Related drug Crimes, Human Trafficking, January 7-April 13, 20009, www.ybnews.cn (May 9, 2009).

139. Carla Freeman, "Fragile Edges Between Security and Insecurity: China's Border Regions," in Rongxing Guo and Carla Freeman (eds.), *Managing Fragile Regions: Method and Application,* (New York, Spring: 2010): 39.

a humanitarian disaster on its border and encouraging North Korea to follow a Chinese style model of economic opening and reform that will serve China's domestic development and security objectives for Jilin and its northeastern region more broadly, as well as the parochial development objectives of its border region. While certainly willing to expand its economic links to North Korea and advantage its own economic interests there, it has shown no evidence of neo-colonial ambitions there. For China events on the Korean peninsula have a direct impact on its own territory and people. While China is unwilling to take the kind of punitive action against North Korea that some US policymakers have advocated-- action that it knows from experience by intransigence at best, including a suspension of bilateral economic exchanges by the DPRK, and at worst by an escalation of threats by Pyongyang-- it will support what it perceives as positive steps toward fostering conditions for regional security cooperation. It is, however, unwilling to move boldly, or to be held accountable for North Korea's own policy choices, preferring instead to encourage change across the Tumen and Yalu Rivers than to catalyze an impossible-to-contain crisis involving its fragile neighbor.

......

-III-

Inner Mongolia and Mongolia

"In the South, there is Shenzhen. In the North, there is Erlian."

Genghis Khan Memorial in Ordos, Inner Mongolia[140]

China and Mongolia—Too Close for Comfort ?

When former Chinese premier Zhu Rongji met with his Mongolian counterpart during the World Summit on

140. Author's photo.

Sustainable Development in 2002, he recalled a Chinese maxim that a close neighbor is preferable to a distant relative. While acknowledging the prospects for deeper economic relations between the two countries, Zhu stressed the importance of their political ties, including enhancing bilateral cooperation in international and regional affairs.[141] Less than a decade later, during Wen Jiabao's visit to the Mongolian capital, the Chinese premier focused on the economic dimension of the two countries' relationship, making several new proposals related to expanding economic and trade cooperation, and notably also emphasizing that not only is Mongolia a close neighbor, China assigns priority to its relationship with Mongolia among its many neighbors. For China, Mongolia looms large on its northern edge, not only because of the sheer length of the two countries' common border—China's longest land border with any single country at 4,677 km—but because of the growing importance of Mongolia's wealth of natural resources to China's growing economy. Just a little more than a decade ago, Mongolia was a country receiving significant international aid with uncertain economic prospects. The extent and development potential of Mongolia's deposits of coal, copper and other minerals had only begun to draw international attention. For Beijing's part, China's leaders were also only beginning to understand the extent to which China's growing economy would come to need imports of raw materials from beyond China's borders, including from Mongolia. In 2002, China's trade with Mongolia largely took the form of small-scale border trade; today China is Mongolia's largest trading partner and a major investor

141. "Premier Zhu Rongji Holds Talks with Mongolian Prime Minister Nabaryn Enkhbayar (7/02/2002)," Embassy of the People's Republic in the Kingdom of Denmark, available at http://dk.china-embassy.org/eng/News/t105505.htm.

in the development of Mongolia's natural resources, with an estimated USD1.011 billion in investment in Mongolia through 2009, principally in Mongolia's mineral resources--making itself Mongolia's biggest foreign investor 12 years in a row. In March 2010, China also made a USD3 billion loan to Mongolia to develop its roads.[142]

The growing importance China now assigns to imports of Mongolian resources have amplified its concerns about other factors that intersect with this expanding economic relationship with its neighbor. Over 5 million ethnic Mongolians live in China's Inner Mongolia— a population significantly larger than that within Mongolia itself. This alone is cause for Beijing about the possible influence of Mongolian nationalism on its own Mongolian population. The potential links between the pan-Mongolian movement and Tibetan Buddhism with its relationship to the politics surrounding the Dalai Lama sharpens this concern. At the level of high politics, China is chary of democratic Mongolia's good relations with the US and its democratic allies in Asia. It remains concerned that, as was the case during the Cold War, Mongolia could once again serve as a base for those who would threaten China, particularly its "three Norths"—North China, Northeast China and Northwest China.[143]

---

142. Migeddorj Batchimeg, "Future Challenges for the PRC and Mongolia: A Mongolia Perspective," China Brief, Volume 5, Issue 10 (May 05, 2005): 4; Fang Hua, "Neighbors and Partners: China and Mongolia Make the Most of their Business Ties," Beijing Review, August 12, 2010: http://www.bjreview.com.cn/world/txt/2010-08/06/content_289316.htm

143. Wang Peiran, "Sino-Mongolian Military Relations," China Security, Vol. 5.2 (2009): 70.

At the same time, China and Mongolia have sought to further regional and subregional cooperation in a broad spectrum of spheres. China has supported Mongolia accession to the Asia Cooperation Dialogue (ACD), Asia-Pacific Economic Community (APEC)-- access to which Mongolia was denied [144]-- and the Asia-Europe Meeting (ASEM), and granting Mongolia observer status in the Shanghai Cooperation Organization's (SCO). China and Mongolia cooperate through other regional groupings as well, such as the Northeast Asia Economic Forum. Mongolia is also member of the Greater Tumen Initiative (GTI) with China, South Korea, and Russia. Three of its aimags (provinces)--Dornod, Hentii and Sukh Bator--are taking part in the project to promote economic cooperation through improved infrastructure linkages, and investment and trade cooperation among provinces or provincial level entities in the Tumen River basin. Until 2009, the project served as a confidence-building mechanism in that North Korea was a regular participant in the GTI, along with China, Russia, South Korea as well as Mongolia. In addition to this security dimension, the GTI has been of particular interest to land-locked Mongolia because of its emphasis on facilitating access to coastal ports, improving logistics, and linking Northern Asian to European markets through expanded rail facilities. The GTI has provided the framework for prospective investment by a company in China's Jilin province, a key participant in the Tumen project,-- the Jilin Sino-Mongolia Railway Energy (Investment and Development), Ltd.--to invest in an expanded Mongolia-China rail link as well as in the mining sector of Eastern Mongolia.[145] China has included this plan as well as another

144.US Department of State, "Mongolia Country Profile," available at http://www.state.gov/r/pa/ei/bgn/2779.htm.

145.Ruslan Gulidov , "Mongolia-China Railway Feasibility Study," April 6, 2010, available at http://www.tumenprogramme.org/news.php?id=482.

new rail project linking Mongolia's Choibalsan to Tongliao and Jinzhou to be constructed by China's Liaoning province in its latest plans to spur development in its own northeastern region, including Inner Mongolia, through the " Chang-Ji-Tu Pilot Zone" project announced in 2009.[146]

Even as the two countries' economic ties deepen, the interwoven history of Chinese and Mongolians has left its own enduring legacies that continue to influence and complicate the contemporary international relationship between China and Mongolia today. For Mongolians, Qing (Manchu) subjugation of their ancestors is remembered bitterly in their historical narratives, even as Mongol nationalists celebrate Mongolia's own expansionist history, including into China. Mongolians continue to worry about the potential for an influx of Chinese into their sparsely inhabited territory as they look southward across their own open grasslands toward China's massive population. And, despite China's assurances that it respects Mongolia's independence and sovereignty, a fear that China could once again seek to annex Mongolia as a "lost Chinese territory" remains very much alive among some Mongolians. In addition, although per capita GDP in Mongolia has grown substantially in the last decade - from about USD350 to USD1550[147]–Mongolia's mining boom has yet to trickle down to much of Mongolia's population, more than a third of which continues to be dependent upon semi-nomadic livestock herding. Unemployment in Ulan Bator also remains

---

146. Yu Xiao, "Study on Changchun-Jilin-Tumen Pilot Zone and International Transport in Tumen River Delta," May 25, 2010, available at www.tumenprogramme.org/news.php?id=864.
147. US Department of State, "Mongolia Country Profile," available at http://www.state.gov/r/pa/ei/bgn/2779.htm

high.[148] Yet, the RMB is widely circulated in Mongolia, called by some the "second Mongolian dollar." For some in Mongolia, China's growing presence on their side of the border appears predatory rather than economically beneficial, a perception that, as will be discussed further below, has become a source of domestic political unrest within Mongolia in recent years.

Shared History

Mongolians were among those "northern barbarians" that the sedentary Han and others within "inner China" feared as a threat to Chinese imperial rule. In 1206 Genghis Khan united the area's nomadic tribes under his control, establishing the Mongol empire, later extending his military reach into Persia, Central Asia and part of European Russia and the Caucuses. His grandson, Kublai Khan, consolidated Mongol control over a vast expanse of territory by conquering China and establishing the Yuan Dynasty (1279-1368AD), the centerpiece of a Mongol empire that at its peak encompassed about a fifth of the world's inhabited land mass.

Following the Yuan dynastic collapse and the rise of first a powerful Ming and then Manchu Qing empire, Mongolians in turn became the subjugated. Dominating and dividing Mongol lands was part of the Manchu rise to power. In 1691, with the Manchus ensconced in Beijing as the Qing much of Mongol territory was formally divided and made into administrative regions of China. Today's "Inner Mongolia" was broken into many different banners and leagues controlled by the Manchu Qing dynasty, which also asserted control over the Buddhist churches that had once been an important source of unity among the Mongols

---

148. Australian government, Export, Finance and Insureance Corporation, December 2010, available at http://efic.com/country/countryprofiles/Pages/Mongolia.aspx.

in the region.[149]

All of Mongolia was conquered in 1757, when Outer Mongolia became a Chinese province. This was the status it would have within the Chinese empire until the fall of the Qing Dynasty in 1911, when Mongolia's nobility declared Mongolian independence from Manchu rule. In the early years of the Chinese Republican government, from 1912-1919, Mongolia retained its autonomy with Russian support. While Russia was engulfed in revolution and civil war, Chinese authorities were able to reincorporate Mongolia into China as a province in 1919. In 1921, however, Russia's now Soviet forces occupied Mongolia's capital and helped Mongolia's own communist revolutionaries win control over "Outer Mongolian" territory. Mongolia established itself as an independent country, the Mongolian People's Republic under the Mongolian People's Revolutionary Party (MPRP), the second country to declare itself a communist state after the Soviet Union.

Despite its de facto autonomy, until the Soviet Union's collapse, for seven decades Mongolia was a client state of the Soviet Union, an unofficial "sixteenth Soviet republic." Reliance on the Soviet Union, including the suppression of traditional Mongolian culture and the replacement of the Sanskrit-based Mongol script by the Cyrillic alphabet, was seen by Mongolia's leadership as preferable to a loss of independence as a result of Chinese intervention.[150] A perceived threat by China to Mongolian independence has endured as the result of a number of factors. The first relate to China's claims to sovereignty over Mongolian territory. Promises of autonomy for Mongolians when seeking

149.Uradyn E. Bulag, "Inner Mongolia: The Dialectics of Colonization and Ethnicity Building," in Morris Rossabi (ed.), Governing China's Multiethnic Frontiers, (Seattle and London: University of Washington Press, 2004): 86.

Mongol support in the Chinese civil war[151] by Mao Zedong were not exclusive of irredentist sentiments by the new Chinese leadership toward all Mongolian territory. In an interview with American reporter, Edgar Snow, Mao had also remarked, echoing alleged comments made two decades earlier by Sun Yatsen: "When the people's revolution has been victorious in China, the Outer Mongolian republic will automatically become a part of the Chinese federation, at their own will." Mao later repeated similar statements to another foreign journalist.[152] Through much of its history, the nationalist Chinese government on Taiwan [Republic of China (R.O.C)] rejected Mongolian independence from China and used its then permanent membership on the UN Security Council to keep Mongolia out of the United Nations throughout the 1950s. Although the government on Taiwan has formally recognized Mongolia's independence since 2002, the official borders of the R.O.C. have yet to be formally changed to exclude Mongolia as R.O.C. territory.

A second driving reason has been nothing less than Inner Mongolia's experience under Chinese control. Despite Inner Mongolia's administrative status within China as an ethnic autonomous region, to greatly oversimplify, Mongolians beyond its border have watched its transformation into a region with a Han-dominated political leadership that has also been overwhelmingly populated by Han Chinese, with its once pastoral regions "modernized" and put under till. More recently, since 2001 hundreds of thousands of nomads and herders have been forcibly relocated to urban

---

150. Tom Ginsburg, "Political Reform in Mongolia: Between Russia and China," Asian Survey, Vol. 35, No. 5 (May, 1995): 460 see also Elizabeth E. Green, "China and Mongolia: Recurring Trends and Prospects for Change,": Asian Survey, Vol. 26, No. 12 (Dec., 1986): 1337-1363.
151. Bulag, (2004): 89.
152. Green, 1342.

areas as part of a program of enclosure linked to grassland restoration.[153]

The fall of the Soviet Union brought with it disastrous consequences for Mongolia, which had been nearly entirely dependent upon its ally for economic subsidies. Without Soviet support, Mongolia's economy faltered. However, even in the face of economic uncertainty, following popular calls for democracy, in March of 1990 the Mongolian communist party peacefully relinquished its ruling status, establishing democratic institutions and legalizing opposition parties ahead of multiparty elections. Elections were held later that year, and a bicameral legislature was elected comprising MPRP representatives alongside those representing a number of opposition parties.[154] In 1992 the Mongolian government promulgated a new constitution, implementing political and economic reforms. By 1996, the power of the once dominant (formerly communist) Mongolian People's Revolutionary Party (MPRP) had been checked by the opposition party, the Mongolian Democratic Party (MDP), which took the majority in Mongolia's 76 seat parliament.[155]

153.Bulag (2004): 100-101; Tim Johnson , "China's Ethnic Mongolians Hang on to Identity by a Thread," Mcclatchy Newspapers, Nov 13,2008, available at chinadigitaltimes. net/.../chinas-ethnic-mongolians-hang-on-to-identity-by-a- thread/ .

154. Daisy Sindelar, "From Mongolian Democracy: From Post-Soviet Success To Post-Transition Struggle," Radio Free Europe, December 9, 2009, available at .http://www.rferl. org/content/Mongolian_Democracy_From_PostSoviet_Success_To_PostTransition_Struggle/1899808.html; see also Ginsburg: 463 .

155.Edward Wong, "In Election Dispute, a Challenge for Mongolia's Democracy," New York Times, July 8, 2008, available at http://www.nytimes.com/2008/07/08/world/asia/08mongolia.html?

After almost two decades as a democracy, however, domestic political tensions threatened to destabilize the country. When it was announced that the MPRP had regained the majority in parliament following elections on June 29, 2008, the leader of the opposition party, T. Elbegdorj, accused the MPRP of election fraud and encouraged his supporters to riot. On July 1, a crowd of 8,000 rioters attacked the MPRP headquarters and the neighboring Mongolian National Art Gallery. When police became involved, clashes led to the death of 5 and arrest of over 700 protesters.[156] The president at the time, Enkhbayar, announced a four day emergency, reportedly the first in Mongolia's history. In the riot's aftermath, media outlets were closed and soldiers patrolled the streets.[157] China figured in these riots: among the protestors' complaints against the MPRP was a claim that the party accepted financing from China (and also Russia) in return for facilitating access to Mongolia's resources. The MPRP was known to have a strong pro-China contingent. Just a week before the elections, Chinese Vice-President Xi Jinping, Hu Jintao's heir apparent, had visited Mongolia, promising additional investment by Chinese companies in infrastructure construction and other development assistance.[158]

There is no question that, as Chinese investment in Mongolia has grown, anti-Chinese feeling has also been on the rise, with the number of xenophobic attacks against Chinese nationals in Mongolia increasing in recent years. Ethnic tensions between the now overwhelmingly Han majority within Inner Mongolia and the region's ethnic

---

156. Edward Wong.
157. Wong.
158. "Mongolian Vote Sparks Riots, Near 'Color Revolution'?" The Current Digest of the Post-Soviet Press, No. 26, Vol.60, July 22, 2008: 8 , available at http://dlib.eastview.com/browse/doc/20437892.

Mongolian population are unquestionably far lower than those in Tibet and Xinjiang, where for one the Han Chinese population remains in the minority. Nonetheless, organized ethnic-nationalism and anti-Chinese feeling exists even among Chinese Mongolians. In 1997, Mongolians from China as well as Mongolia and other countries held a "Global Mongolian Clansmen Plenary Session," to focus on organizing an Inner Mongolian nationalist liberation movement. The outcome with the establishment of an "Inner Mongolian People's Party" (in Chinese "neiren dang") with the goal of ending "Chinese occupation" of Inner Mongolia "and "stop[ping] Chinese immigration and population assimilation policies toward Mongols."[159] The neiren dang deliberately hearkens to the former Inner Mongolian People's Party, a party founded with Soviet support in the 1920s, whose alleged "splittest" objectives prompted a brutal campaign by Maoists against purported members during the period of the Sino-Soviet split.[160]

According to one source, 17% of Inner Mongolia's Mongolian population adhered to the party in 2005.[161] A "Southern Mongolian Democratic Alliance," a group with the mission of promoting Mongolian cultural values in Inner Mongolia also operates outside Inner Mongolia.

China frames its relationship with Mongolia today in terms that are consistent with those it generally applies to its international relationships with other smaller states

---

159. "Inner Mongolian People's Party" website: http://www.innermongolia.org/english/index.html.

160. David Sneath, "The Impact of the Cultural Revolution in China on the Mongolians of Inner Mongolia," Modern Asian Studies, Vol. 28, No. 2 (May, 1994): 421.

161. Wang Wei-Fang, "Pan-Mongolism and U.S.-China-Mongolia relations," Association for Asian Research, June 29, 2005, available at http://www.asianresearch.org/articles/2644.html.

along its borders. It seeks a "neighborly and mutual-trusting partnership"[162] through an emphasis on the cooperative aspects of the bilateral relationship, and reassuring Mongolia that it will respect Mongolian sovereignty. In rhetoric surrounding its "good neighbor" relationship with Mongolia, China emphasizes its early recognition of Mongolia as an independent state, having officially established diplomatic relations with Ulan Bator in 1949, as well as its efforts to resolve mutual border dispute, resulting in a 1962 treaty whereby it relinquished its claims on around 12,000 square kilometers of the territory of its then "fraternal" socialist neighbor.[163]

When the political turmoil of the Cultural Revolution subsided and Sino-Soviet tensions thawed, efforts were made on both China and Mongolia's sides to further develop the relationship. In July of 1984 a delegation from Ulan Bator met with China's Minister of Foreign Affairs in Beijing to discuss expanding the bilateral relationship. A first step was reaffirming sovereign borders; that meeting resulted in a document substantiating the first joint inspection of the China-Mongolian border. However, the continuing presence of Soviet troops in Mongolia—with Mongolia's support—thwarted progress in China's relationship with Mongolia. Relations improved after Gorbachev's 1986 speech announcing possible troops withdrawals and the visit of a Mongolia Vice foreign minister to Beijing, which resulted in the signing of a consular agreement between the two countries followed by a treaty on a border control system

162."China-Mongolia Relations," China Daily, May 25, 2010, available at http://www.chinadaily.com.cn/china/2010wentour/2010-05/27/content_9899648.htm.

163. M. Taylor Fravel, "Regime Insecurity and International Cooperation Explaining China's Compromises in Territorial Disputes," International Security: Vol. 30, No. 2 (Fall 2005): 72; 73, available at http://www.gwu.edu/~power/literature/dbase/fravel1.pdf.

between the two countries in 1988. Beijing's eagerness to begin to improve relations with Ulan Bator despite the latter's unwillingness to change its position on the continuing need for a Soviet military presence on its territory was certainly aided by the dramatic improvement in United States-Mongolia relations, which resulted in mutual recognition in 1987. Numerous diplomatic exchanges followed; however, bilateral relations were normalized only in 1989 amid the collapse of the Soviet Union.[164]

A desire to resolve political and security tensions and to ensure that Mongolia's improved relations with the US would not crowd out Beijing's own opportunities for better relations with Ulan Bator underlay the early focus on settling borders and the reduction of Soviet troops stationed in Mongolia between the two sides. However, expanding trade was also an important driver of the decision by both countries to take early steps to re-constitute bilateral relations. After years of dependency on Moscow's largesse, Mongolia was aware that its reduced significance in Moscow's security calculations would reduce the economic support it would receive and it sought to diversify its economic partnerships.

To say that bilateral trade between the two sides has exceeded expectations is an understatement. Total trade turnover between the two countries at USD2.8 billion in 2008 was 18 times its level in 1990.[165] China has been

---

164. U.S. Library of Congress, "Mongolia Country Studies," October 8, 2010, available at http://countrystudies.us/mongolia/65.htm.; Kerry Dumbaugh and Wayne M. Morrison," Congressional Research Service, (7-5700, June 18, 2009): 1.

165. J. Shishmishig, "Current Situation of Mongolia-China Trade Cooperation and Further Trends," (2009): (http://www.adb.org/Documents/Events/2009/Joint-Dissemination-ZamynUud-Erlian/MON-PRC-Cooperation.pdf).

Mongolia's number one trading partner for the past 11 years; in 2009 it made up 36% of Mongolia's imports and 79% of its exports.[166] China sells Mongolia basic foodstuffs and goods from rice and vegetables to clothing, as well as electronics, machinery, and construction goods associated with Mongolia's own construction boom, in addition to offering its land-locked country neighbor port access at Tianjin.[167] China imports coal, metals, and oil from Mongolia.[168] Trade grew over 20 percent from 2009 to 2010 and in 2010 the two sides began exploring the possibility of a free-trade agreement.[169] Foreign investment flows both ways across the border. China has over 5000 firms of various sizes in Mongolia, with investment totaling over $1 billion,

166."Border Town bustling with business as Sino-Mongolia trade takes off," Xinhua, June 1, 2010, available at http://www.chinadaily.com.cn/bizchina/2010-06/01/content_9919141.htm ; "Mongolia: EU Bilateral Trade and With the World," September 15, 2010, available at http://trade.ec.europa.eu/doclib/docs/2006/september/tradoc_113420.pdf.

167. 'Steady Growth in China-Mongolia trade, economic co-op," China View, June 19, 2008, available at http://news.xinhuanet.com/english/2008-06/19/content_8399506.htm; See also: "Border Town bustling with business as Sino-Mongolia trade takes off," Xinhua, June 1, 2010, available at http://www.chinadaily.com.cn/bizchina/2010-06/01/content_9919141.htm.

168. "Border Town bustling with Business as Sino-Mongolia trade takes off," Xinhua, June 1, 2010, available at http://www.chinadaily.com.cn/bizchina/2010-06/01/content_9919141.htm.
availableathttp://www.chinadaily.com.cn/bizchina/2010-06/01/content_9919141.htm.

169. "The Asian Wolf bites the hand of opportunity," China Daily, September 13, 2010, available at http://www.chinadaily.com.cn/cndy/2010-09/13/content_11291548.htm.

70% of this in mining.[170] Investment from Mongolia itself to China, however, remains very limited, with only 40 of its firms active inside China.[171]

High-Level Exchanges; Chinese leaders visiting Mongolia

Name	Year
Premier Zhou Enlai	1954
National Vice Chairman Zhu De	1956
Premier Zhou Enlai	1960
President Yang Shangkun	1991
Premier Li Peng	1994
NPC Standing Committee Chairman Qiao Stone	1997
Deputy Premier and Foreign Minister Qian Qichen	1997
President Jiang Zemin	1999
The CPC Central Committee, secretary of the Secretariat Wei Jianxing	2000
President Hu Jintao	2003
Deputy Premier Wu Yi	2005
CPPCC National Committee Vice Chairman Xu Kuangi	2006
Vice President Xi Jinping	2008
Premier Wen Jiabao	2010

Source: http://world.huanqiu.com/roll/2010-05/826809.htm

170. Zhang Jin, "China supports firms investing in Mongolia," China Daily, June 2, 2010, available at http://www.chinadaily.com.cn/china/2010-06/02/content_9922257.htm.
171. Shishmishig (2009).

China has sought to undergird its economic relationship with Mongolia with security cooperation. In July of 2009 Chinese and Mongolian forces took part in a joint military peacekeeping exercise with 45 soldiers from each side meeting for nearly a week of training at a base in Beijing. This was China's first peacekeeping exercise with a foreign country, and the first joint military exercise between China and Mongolia. [172] Nearly a year earlier, in September 2008, perhaps also timed to coincide with the annual multinational peacekeeping exercise involving the United States and Mongolia with other countries that month, China ran a "Sharpening 2008" military drill in Inner Mongolia, including more than 5,000 troops from the Beijing Military Area Command and Jinan Military Area Command, as well as the Air Force.[173] Suren Baasankhuu, Vice Defense Minister of Mongolia attended the war game.[174] Since 2004, the two countries have held an Annual Defense Security Consultation.[175] China has supplied Mongolia with equipment to develop construction battalions.[176] China has also sought to expand and improve frontier defense cooperation with Mongolia; Mongolian servicemen have

---

172."China, Mongolia launch joint peacekeeping exercise," Xinhua, June 28, 2009, available at http://news.xinhuanet.com/english/2009-06/28/content_11615899.htm.

173. Uradyn Erden Bulag, "Mongolia in 2008: From Mongolia to Mine-golia," Asian Survey, Vol. 49, Issue 1 (2009): 134.

174. "Foreign Officers Observe China's Latest War Game," Xinhua, September 26, 2008, available at http://english.cri.cn/2946/2008/09/26/168s409329.htm.

175. "China, Mongolia explore new fields in military co-op," Xinhua, August 20, 2010, (http://www.chinadaily.com.cn/china/2010-08/20/content_11182766.htm).

176. S. Batbayar, " China delivers construction equipment for Mongolian military," BBC Worldwide Monitoring, February 28, 2010.

participated in training activities in China.[177]

Inner Mongolia in China-Mongolian Relations: "Rainbow" Bridge— and Barrier

Within the China-Mongolia relationship, Inner Mongolia plays both a pivotal and multifaceted role. Not only is it the conduit for much of China's trade with Mongolia, its own traders and investors are also important players in Mongolia, as well as in the "gray" cash economy that has constituted a significant share of Mongolia's unmeasured economy even in recent years.[178] Chinese authorities have also sought to use Inner Mongolia as a cultural bridge to undergird China's diplomatic relationship with Mongolia and advantage Chinese economic interests there, amid intensifying international competition for Mongolia's minerals. While the clash between Mongolian cultural norms and the pattern of Chinese development alone has made this difficult, cultural affinities have fostered local cooperation across the border. Chinese ethnic-Mongolian traders are active in cross-border trade. However, in volume and scale Inner Mongolia's economic interactions with Mongolia are dominated such massive companies as its Baotou Steel. The celebration of Mongol nationalism across the border in Mongolia, with its tinges of anti Chinese feeling, as well as within the Mongolian diaspora has intensified Beijing's concerns that the autonomous region they have long regarded as a "model" one could see ethnically-focused discontent. Ethnic Mongolians in Inner

177. B. Huder, "Mongolian PM, Chinese general praise Defence Cooperation," BBC Worldwide Monitoring, August 19, 2010;, available at http://english.chinamil.com.cn/site2/news-channels/2007-07/13/content_879579.htm. 07/13/content_879579.htm.

178. US Department of State, "Mongolia Country Profile," available at http://www.state.gov/r/pa/ei/bgn/2779.htm

Mongolia remain economically less well off than their Han Chinese compatriots and have found it difficult to preserve not only their pastoral way of life but their language as well, social and economic conditions associated with conflict along ethnic lines.

China's border with Mongolia accounts for over 20% of China's land borders. The majority of the Sino-Mongolian border runs along Inner Mongolia. Chinese analysts often describe Inner Mongolia as a "rainbow" for its multi dimensional role bridging China and Mongolia through trade, transborder, and cultural ties.[179] As if to bring this rainbow theme to life, the border crossing at Inner Mongolia's most important border port with Mongolia, Erlian (also "Eren," which means "colorful" in Mongolian), is adorned with rainbow archways.

Inner Mongolia is the front gate for economic relations between China and Mongolia. Of the goods transported between the two countries, 80% flow through Inner Mongolia's nine border ports.[180] Erlian is the largest of these

179."""" – –," China.org, March 2, 2005, available at http://www.china.com.cn/book/zhuanti/qkjc/txt/2005-03/02/content_5799738.htm.

180. "," Xinhua, May 3, 2010, available at http://www.nmg.xinhuanet.com/ldhd/2010-05/03/content_20234070.htm.

trading ports and only rail connection to Mongolia on the China-Mongolian border; more than 70% of Sino-Mongolian trade flows through Erlian, in Xin Gol League ( ). This part of North-central Inner Mongolia has an ethnic Mongolian population that is about 30% of its total, nearly twice the percentage of ethnic Mongolians in Inner Mongolia as a whole.

Erlian has had city status since 1966 due to its increased importance after the opening of the Trans-Mongolian railway connecting Beijing-Ulan Bator-Moscow in the mid-1950s. It was further elevated to a prefecture level city in 1985, just months after the resumption of diplomatic contact between Ulan Bator and Beijing. [181] Its importance in cross-border activity between China and Mongolia is evidenced by the existence of a Mongolian consulate in the city since 1996. The route from Erlian is the only railway into Mongolia from China, and only 9 km separate Erlian from Zamyn-Uud, its dusty counterpart on the Mongolian side of the border, clearly visible from the outskirts of Erlian. Inadequate customs and inspection facilities in Zamyn-Uud to handle the surge in cross-border trade has led to congestion and bottlenecks in cross border trade. In late 2010, the Asian Development Bank announced that it had lent the government of Mongolia USD45 million to construct a container terminal with transportation links to relieve bottlenecks at the border.[182] China and Mongolia have begun meeting regularly to try to harmonize customs procedures and with ADB support have convened representatives of appropriate ministries on both sides

181. "," Sinotrans-el, available at http://www.sinotrans-el.com/kagk.php.

182. " ADB Funds Logistics Center to Help Mongolia Expand, Speed Up Trade," The Financial, available at http://finchannel.com/Main_News/Business/77497_ADB_Funds_Logistics_Center_to_Help_Mongolia_Expand,_Speed_Up_Trade/.

and leaders in border cooperation efforts, such as from the Inner Mongolian government in Hohhot and the director of Erlian Border Economic Cooperation Management[183] to explore ways to further coordinate and develop of a joint border commission.[184]

On the Chinese side, PBWM funds have helped under write development of some of the infrastructure to facilitate cross-border trade through improving transportation, expanding the already overtaxed rail system, facilitating customs processes through upgraded equipment and staff training, and promoting energy conservation.[185] Erlian also received funding to construct an Erlian airport with flights to Hohhot and Beijing. Following successful trial runs in late 2009, the airport formally began operations in early 2010. In the future flights will extend to Shanghai, Mongolia, and Russia.[186] In addition, road construction has proceeded apace, with the completion of several new highways during the Eleventh Five Year plan period, including a national "208" highway. [187]

183.Joint Dissemination Workshop on the Study of Zamyn-Uud and Erlian Border Development Program, (Inner Mongolia Autonomous Region (IMAR), PRC, April 14, 2009, Hohhot, available at http://www.carecinstitute.org/uploads/events/2009/Joint-PRC-MON-Dissemination/Joint-Dissemination-Program.pdf.

184. D.Oyunchimeg, "Country Report, Mongolia Customs: Achievements made during 2001-2010 under the CAREC Program," available at http://www.carecinstitute.org/uploads/events/2010/9th-CCC/Customs-Progress-Report-MON.pdf.

185." ," People.com.cn, August 10, 2009, (http://politics.people.com.cn/GB/14562/9828474.html)..

186. , ," Inner Mongolia Journal, August 5, 2010, available at http://www.nmrb.cn/Item/232560.aspx.

187. ""," ,December 10, 2010, available at http://www.elht.gov.cn/.

Border crossing is relatively easy for local traders who regularly traverse the border. They can use entry-exit passes, which are inspected on the Chinese side of the border at the "Frontier Inspection Station," staffed by China's public security border force. Chinese traders in goods like fruits and vegetables from Erlian, some ethnic Mongolian, work with Mongolian business partners across the border to ship their products via train at Zamyn-Uud to Ulan Bator, more than 650 km to the Northwest. On Erlian's streets, cars with Mongolian license plates are intermingled with those registered in Inner Mongolia. The growing volume of people moving across the border daily along with sustained poverty, unemployment and drug use in Mongolia and the lure of China's booming economy has also made it easier in recent years for human traffickers to use Erlian as a transport route. Mongolian women destined for the sex trade and both adults and children targeted for forced labor are increasingly trafficked into China using the relatively unregulated channel of overseas labor recruitment.[188]

Fiscal Flows: Prosperous Borders, Wealthy Minorities

Rising cross-border trade has led to rapid population growth in Erlian, and it and its environs receive substantial central fiscal transfers for infrastructure and poverty alleviation. PBWM programs have contributed to the development of basic infrastructure at the local level, including the development of wells, trash systems, public toilets, schools, health institutions as well as on improvements to schools. For example, Erlian authorities spent RMB1,400,000 on upgrading local school facilities, including the construction of libraries, computer rooms,

188.B. Bulgamaa, "Study: Mongolia Must Battle Increase in Human Trafficking," UB Post, January 22, 2009: ," available at http://ubpost.mongolnews.mn/index.php?option=com_content&task=view&id=2578&Itemid=36.

and gyms.[189] With parts of Xinjiang and Tibet and several other minority regions, Erlian has also received funding from another central government program, the "New West project," to extend both radio and television service to its population. [190] Central government funds have been also targeted local projects to reduce over-grazing, including by providing local herdsmen free housing for five years providing they relocate to nearby towns.[191] The city of Beijing, which receives a large share of its power from Inner Mongolia, is also a source of development assistance.

Similar changes on the Mongolian side of the border associated with expanded mining and trade have not met with an adequate government response. The ADB recently approved project funding for border town development and local government capacity building in the region.[192] To date, however, China has sought to manage cross-border pressures and promote good Sino-Mongolian relations drawing on PBWM funding through such projects as a RMB1,000,000 PBWM China-Mongolia friendship hospital, for example.[193] With support from Hohhot, they have set up an international language school to help the many Mongolian students who reside in Erlian learn Chinese. There are additional plans to build a Mongol minority

---

189. "," August10, 2009, <http://cd.qq.com/a/20090810/002142.htm> (21 September 2010).
190. "","" ,(12-10-2010), (http://www.elht.gov.cn/).
191. Manzhouli Government, "," October 26, 2009, available at http://manzhouli.gov.cn/info/InfoContent.aspx?c_id=1253.
192. "Southeast Gobi and Border Town Development Project," Asian Development Bank, available at www.adb.org/Documents/Reports/Consultant/.../42184-MON-TACR.pdf.
193. "," August 10, 2009, available at http://cd.qq.com/a/20090810/002142.htm.

school.[194] These efforts are encouraged by central authorities who remain concerned that local development and the cross-border trade that is so vital to it could be disrupted by cultural tensions in particular. A recent CCTV-9 program on Erlian featuring the interaction between a local ethnic Mongolian trader in Erlian and her Mongolian partner in Zamyn-Uud stressed the cooperation between the two groups of Mongolians, including showing Mongolian children attending school in Erlian also sharing in a local Mongolian sporting event on the outskirts of Erlian, which "teaches the children about the traditional Mongolian way of life." The narrator observes that these interactions are symbols of the way that today "people of the same ethnic group but who are living on two sides of a frontier have been reunited through border trade."[195]

The broadcast points to an important and complicated aspect of the China-Mongolian relationship in which Inner Mongolia also plays a role: that of cultural exchange. There are of course the regular cultural interchanges of traditional diplomacy. In 2004 Mongolia began hosting an annual "Chinese Cultural Week," and a parallel annual "Mongolian Culture Week" began in China in 2005. In May of 2008 a Confucius Institute for Mandarin instruction was established at the National University of Mongolia. During Wen's 2010 visit to Ulan Bator, the Chinese premier also stressed the importance of cultural exchanges, and stated that the Chinese government will grant scholarships to 2000 Mongolian students in the next five years.[196] A direct

---

194. "," August 10, 2009, available at http://cd.qq.com/a/20090810/002142.htm.
195. "The City of Erlian Haote on the Chinese Mongolian Border," CCTV-9, May 9, 2009.
196. "China, Mongolia agree to boost cooperation in energy, trade," People's Daily Online, June 2, 2010, available at http://english.peopledaily.com.cn/90001/90776/90883/7008278.html.

agreement (referred to as a treaty on the Mongolian Ministry of Education, Culture and Science website) between Inner Mongolia and Mongolia implemented in 2008 builds on earlier educational programs supporting study by Mongolians in China, enabling 170 Mongolian students to enroll in a range of undergraduate and graduate universities and programs, in Chinese.[197] There are fewer opportunities for Chinese to study in Mongolia, however. While university exchanges are not uncommon, Mongolia maintains some of Northeast Asia's most restrictive policies on immigration.[198]

China has also sought to engage with Mongolia through Mongolian culture as well. The two countries signed a Cultural Cooperation Agreement in 1994. But, this has at times proven counterproductive from the perspective of Chinese interests, as these efforts have often become entangled in Mongol nationalism and pan-nationalism. For example, as Mongolia has fitfully attempted a return to using Mongolian script and a move away from the Cyrillic writing system it had adopted in the 1940s, Mongolian studies centers in Inner Mongolia have presented potential resources. Indeed, western students of Mongolian generally study Mongolian in Inner Mongolia. Mongolian Language and Script Discipline is a key program of Inner Mongolia University's International College of Education; Menksoft is an Inner Mongolian software company with close links to Inner Mongolia University that developed software for the Mongolian script. The idea that China has "preserved" the

---

197. Mongolian Ministry of Education, Culture and Science website, available at http://www.mongolweb.net/edu/index.php?songolt=content&task=content_item&id=219&menu_id=53%5C'

198. Tsuneo Akata, "Transborder Migration in Northeast Asia and Policy Agenda," 2010 PCRD International Conference, available at http://www.region.go.kr/jeju_conference/SESSION2_1.pdf.

Mongolian language is fraught with irony, however, to some of Mongolian heritage. Scholar and critic of Chinese policies toward Inner Mongolia Bulag has written poignantly about the loss of Mongolian language in Inner Mongolia due to Han settlement and what he calls the "domestication" of Mongolian and the disruption of its linguistic diversity as part of China's Maoist-era nationalities policy.[199] Some Mongolians acknowledge that Inner Mongolia offers a repository of many Mongolian traditions and artifacts, such as The Secret History of the Mongols, a 14th century Chinese transcription of a 13th century Mongolian history of the life of Genghis Khan. However, many are galled by assertions by Chinese that its Inner Mongolian universities and research institutes make "China ... the leading center of Mongolian studies in the world[,]" as a piece in Xinhua declared some years ago.[200]

Despite the critical view many Mongolians have of China's management of ethnic Mongolian affairs, there has been some cooperation with China to try to preserve Mongolian traditions. The "Secret History" and other materials related to Mongol history and culture are objects of study by scholars from Mongolia, who engage with their Chinese and Chinese Mongolian counterparts. Universities in Inner Mongolia have formal relationships for cultural as well as other forms of cooperation (such as the provision of technical assistance in the area of agriculture)[201] with the National University of Mongolia, and there is regularly scholarly exchange between Inner Mongolia and other

199. Uradyn E. Bulag, "Mongolian Ethnicity and Linguistic Anxiety in China," American Anthropologist, Volume 5, Issue 4 (December 2003): 756.

200. http://www.newsgd.com/culture/culturenews/200508230020.htm

201. http://www.mongolia-investment.com/news/political-news/37-chinese-and-russian-scholars-arrive

Chinese scholars of Mongolian culture and history and Mongolia. There are also formal cultural preservation endeavors: in 2007, for example, the two countries agreed to work together to preserve the dying art of the Mongolian "long song."[202] After Mongolian citizens organized protests against China's registration of "khoomi," Mongolian throat singing, as an aspect of its cultural heritage with UNESCO, Mongolian officials worked to reach a compromise with China, agreeing when UNESCO later its procedures to allow for more than one country to register so-called "intangible cultural heritage" that they share, to register jointly with China.[203]

'Greater Mongolia' and Pan-Mongolism

For historical background to this discussion and the link between these assertions on the one hand of cultural ownership by Mongolia and China and pan-Mongol sentiment on the other some discussion of Ulanhu Bulag (1906-1988) is required. Ulanhu's story resonates with the entire Mongol community and highlights both the cultural links and cultural mistrust between China and Mongolia. Ulanhu was ethnically Mongolian (though non-Mongolian speaker) Chinese Communist Party official who governed Inner Mongolia as the top CPC official from 1947-1966. For this service is often referred to as the "founder of Inner Mongolia." He rose through the ranks as an alternate member of the politburo, the Deputy Chairman of the National People's Congress, and China's Vice President.

202."Mongolia and China Pledge to Protect Long-song Singing," September 4, 2007, Mongolia-Web, available at http://www.mongolia-web.com/government-and-politics/1346-mongolia-and-china-pledge-to-protect-long-song-singing.

203."UNESCO permits Mongolia to register Khuumii jointly with China, News English, November 17, 2010, available at http://english.news.mn/content/23627.shtml.

In the history of the Communist Party of China (CPC) he is the ethnic minority to have held the highest Party rank. He is highly regarded in both China and Mongolia: in China for his role in leading Mongolian support for China's revolutionary movement and struggle against Japan and helping to unify Mongolia within a single administrative entity, and in Mongolia for his commitment to the rights of Mongols and other minorities within China.[204]

While Ulanhu was initially successful in achieving the territorial reconstitution of Inner Mongolia from the pieces it had been carved into from its previous rulers, he did little to prevent the massive influx of Han Chinese into the region. This ultimately eroded the opportunity for Mongolians within China to press for greater cultural autonomy. Within the first decade of the PRC, more than 3.4 million Han Chinese moved into Inner Mongolia from other parts of China or were incorporated into Inner Mongolia as a result of the reincorporation of territory into Inner Mongolia administrative territory. First anti-Rightist campaign attacks on policies designed to support minority autonomy, followed by new objectives for China's ethnic minorities rooted in Marxist theory aimed at "amalgamating" (ronghe) ethnic groups and Cultural Revolutionary attacks on the Inner Mongolian ethnic leadership and intellectuals resulted in further setbacks for Inner Mongolian autonomy. According to some estimates, more than 20,000 Mongols were killed during the Cultural Revolution.[205] In 1969, amid

---

204. Uradyn Erden Bulag, The Mongols at China's Edge: History and Politics of National Unity (Rowman & Littlefield, 2002): 229-30; "Ulanhu, 82, a Mongol Who Rose To High Posts in Beijing, Is Dead, New York Times, December 9, 1998: http://query.nytimes.com/gst/fullpage.html?res=940DE7DD153AF93AA35751C1A96E948260).

205. Bulag in Rossabi:

heightening tensions between China and the Soviet Union, half of Inner Mongolia's territory was again broken out of the region and divided among neighboring provinces.[206]

It is in no small part because of these experiences that a sense of Mongol identity persists in Inner Mongolia, with some in the region supporting the Pan-Mongol movement that has its strongest advocates within Mongolia itself. Pan Mongolism played a role in the political movements that led to Mongolia's democratization. In 1990, the Mongolian Democratic Party's platform included a call to "unite" the "three Mongolias" (Mongolia, Inner Mongolia, and Mongolian Buryatskaya), promoting a vision of a formal political union among these regions and Mongolian Xinjiang with a unified spoken and written language, to create a "Great Mongolia."[207]

Religion has also played a role in Pan-Mongol identity. Buddhism has been revived in Mongolia in the past two decades after its ban by Mongolia's then communist government in 1937, with Buddhist symbols incorporated into the national emblems of Mongolia's post-communist government to reconstruct Mongolian national identity.[208] In Inner Mongolia, many of the Tibetan Buddhist monasteries that were among Maoists targets have been reconstructed, and monks now populate them once again. In Inner Mongolia, as elsewhere in China, Buddhist practice is state managed, however. The suppression of religious freedom has been a point around which overseas Tibetans

---

206.Sneath: 423; also Joakim Enwall, 'Inter-ethnic relations in Mongolia and Inner Mongolia', Asian Ethnicity, 11: 2 (2010): 243.

207. Wang (2005). Kalmkiya is also sometimes included in the vision of pan-Mongol unity.

208.Tibetan Museum Society page, available at http://www.tibetan-museum-society.org/java/arts-culture-Buddhism-in-Mongolia-After-1990.jsp.

and Inner Mongolians have joined together in criticizing China in such fora as the Unrepresented Nations and Peoples Organization (UNPO). Historically, Tibetan Buddhism has been an inherent aspect of Mongolian cultural identity, with Buddhism becoming the object of state patronage. Advocates for a democratic government in Mongolia in the late 1980s also built support by calling for the "the revival of traditional Mongolian culture, reintroduction of the old Mongolian script, rehabilitation of Genghis [Chinggis] Khan and encouragement to Buddhism."[209] The frequent trips of the Dalai Lama to Mongolia (five visits since 1990) have been met with anger by the Chinese and have created tensions between the two countries.[210] After the Dalai Lama's visit to Mongolia in 1992, for example, Chinese authorities retaliated by temporarily stopping train traffic to and from Mongolia at the border.[211] There is thus through Tibetan Buddhism also a linkage for Chinese policymakers between Tibetan issues and ethnic Mongolian affairs.

Popular culture has also entered into this dynamic. Chinese commercialization of Genghis Khan and his mausoleum in Inner Mongolia had been resisted by local Mongolians who had seen it as degrading to their heritage. At the time, in 2004, Hurd, a popular rock group from

---

209. Sharad K. Soni, "Buddhist Factor in Promoting Traditional Culture in Mongolia," available at http://www.budcon.com/index.php?option=com_content&view=article&id=255%3Abuddhist-factor-in-promoting-traditional-culture-inmongolia&catid=47%3Aarticles&Itemid=117&lang=ru

210. Nomi Morris, "Buddhism continues to flower in Mongolia," Los Angeles Times, September 11, 2010 , available at http://articles.latimes.com/2010/sep/11/local/la-me-beliefs-20100911/3.

211. Morris Rossabi, Modern Mongolia: from Khans to Commissars to Capitalists (University of California Press, 2005): 241.

Mongolia that appeared to share these views was to perform in Hohhot. China barred the group from appearing, with the implication that it was concerned about a surge in Mongolian nationalism on its side of the border.[212] As a visit to the site made clear, the battle against commercialization was lost; Genghis Khan has been commoditized and fit into the historical narrative preferred by Beijing.[213]

Exchanges of government officials, not only at the high level described above, but across the China-Mongolia mutual border is a routine part of the relationship. Mongolia opened a consulate in Hohot more than two decades ago, and Inner Mongolia has had an Office of Trade and Investment in Ulan Bator since 1990s. The Inner Mongolia-Mongolia relationship has even been formalized since 2004 through a high-level summit mechanism. [214] Local delegations from Inner Mongolia visiting Mongolian government offices are routine. Typical of these exchanges was the June 2010 visit of Hu Chunhua, the Inner Mongolia's First Party Secretary, who traveled to Ulan Bator to meet with Miyegombo Enkhbol, the Mongolian Deputy Prime Minister to discuss a range of issues, including expanding cooperation in

---

212. Morris Rossabi, "Introduction: Genghis Khan: World Conqueror?" available at http://www.blackwellpublishing.com/content/BPL_Images/Content_store/Sample_chapter/9780631189497/GK_sample_chap.pdf: 18.
213. Visit by author, May 2008; the transformation of the site can be usefully viewed through the lens of minority representation in China in the context of a constructed national identity explored by Dru Gladney in "Representing Nationality in China: Refiguring Majority/Minority Identities," The Journal of Asian Studies (53.1, February 1994): 92-123..
214. """ – –," China.org, March 2, 2005, available at http://www.china.com.cn/book/zhuanti/qkjc/txt/2005-03/02/content_5799738.htm.

the areas of education, infrastructure, agriculture, trade, borders and environment.[215] China and Mongolia have also engaged in high-level talks to improvement cooperation on law enforcement and security, with an emphasis on cross border crimes.[216] The two sides have sought to improve coordination between local law enforcement personnel as well, with regular meetings between the Zamyn-Uud police and Erlian police departments initiated in 2009.[217]

Reconquest by Connections?

A recent study drawing on images from Google Earth of China's construction of roads and additional railroad routes produced by an environmental consultancy based in Ulan Bator asserts that these Chinese transportation networks will have an environmental and cultural impact about which Mongolian citizens are as yet unaware:

> Our study is a wakeup call to Mongolians to respond to what we believe is the biggest challenge the country has ever faced. Shorn of its once impregnable

---

215."Chinese Inland Province, Mongolia vow to expand ties," People's Daily Online, June 23, 2010, available at http://english.peopledaily.com.cn/90001/90776/90883/7036067.html.

216."China, Mongolia Eye Closer Cooperation on Law Enforcement," People's Daily (English), (December 14, 2010): (http://english.people.com.cn/90001/90776/90883/7231147.html).

217."Human Trafficking in Mongolia," ttp://www.humantrafficking.mn/index.php?cont=2&type=1&lang=0; Police Officer Works to Change Attitudes About Trafficking: Major Tumensbayar is linchpin in anti-trafficking efforts in Mongolia,"America.gov, available at http://www.america.gov/st/democracyhrenglish/2008/June/20080606103008ajesrom0.0239374.html.

> natural barriers to the west, south and east, how can Mongolia keep its culture and natural heritage? Mongolian society has to decide how to respond or events outside will dictate the shape of the nation for better or worse, and act, and act quickly.[218]

The study makes the case that Mongolia's former isolation from China as a result of the two countries' relatively uninhabited and inaccessible border lands is soon to be over. Three border regions in Mongolia are close enough to China that trucks can connect to China's national expressways within no more than an hour of crossing the border.[219] Many trucks are already simply traveling across makeshift roads across fragile desert ecosystems to haul coal or minerals into China. The study argues that it is not so much construction of roads and other transportation networks to access Mongolian minerals by China that Mongolia should be concerned about; rather it is China's own infrastructure development on its side of the border to manage its own resources, people and defense that will have an impact on Mongolia. Mongolia's periphery, the study argues, will now interconnect to China's periphery, integrating Mongolia's southern border regions into China in a way that challenges Mongolia's sovereign control over their destiny.[220] The implication is thus that, while Mongolia's political leaders may seek to limit the country's economic dependence on China by connecting the Tavan Tolgoi coal mine, the world's largest, to Russia via rail rather China, this will have only a limited real effect. The better policy option, the study's authors argue, is to strategically develop rail routes on the Mongolian side

---

218.Robin Grayson and Chimed-Erdene Baatar, "Remote Sensing of Cross-Border Routes between Mongolia and China," World Placer Journal, Vol. 9 (2009), (http://www.mine.mn/WPJ9_3_Cross_Border_Routes.pdf): 3.

219. Grayson and Baatar, 5.

220. Grayson and Baatar, 62.

that will limit road access-- and thus constrain road links to China, while requiring assessments of and public disclosure and consultations on border and trans-boundary impacts of mining and other new developments.[221]

Mongolia, China and US-Mongolian Relations

Sparsely populated countries with fungible natural resources such as Mongolia, inhabited by a mere 3 million people, normally do not factor into the foreign policy calculations of major states. Mongolia does not loom large in U.S. security strategy in Asia. U.S. priorities are on managing relations with China and maintaining its alliances in the region. Furthermore, Mongolia has no relevance to maritime security issues which are priority concerns of all the other nations in Northeast and Southeast Asia. However in recent years, Mongolia's position has not deterred it from reaching out to other countries and developing its, "Third Neighbors" strategy illuminated in its 1994, "Mongolia White Paper on Foreign Affairs."[222] In addition to preserving its ties with China and Russia, Mongolia aims to extend its bilateral relationships with other countries as well, namely the US, Japan, South Korea, and Western Europe. To a large extent this policy has been successful, as more countries have come to regard Mongolia as an important link in the region.[223]

221.Joshua Kucera, "Wary of Chinese Intentions, Mongolia Opts for More Expensive Rail Development," Mad Corporate Services, August 24, 2010: http://www.madmongolia.com/news/mongolia-news/waryofchinese-intentionsmongolia-opts-for-more expensive-rail-development-plan-2402; Grayson and Baatar, 66.

222.Wei-fang Wang, "Mongolia's Role between the US and China," January 18, 2006, available at http://www.mtac.gov.tw/mtacbooke/upload/09501/0202/e2.pdf.

223. Wei-fang Wang, (2006).

Mongolia's strategic location carries importance not just for its two neighbors, but for other countries in the region as well, including the United States. The United States and Mongolia normalized relations in 1987. Following Mongolia's democratic transition and its subsequent attempts to improve relations with other countries, the ties between the two have blossomed. The growing importance the United States attaches to Mongolia is highlighted by President Bush's visit to Mongolia in November of 2005, marking the first visit of a US President to Mongolia. Between 1991 and 2003 the United States provided Mongolia with over $140 million in aid, much of it with the intent to build up Mongolia's military and increase its anti-terrorism capabilities.[224] Mongolia has demonstrated its interest in strengthening ties to the US by supplying troops to international peacekeeping efforts in Iraq and Afghanistan.[225]

In the wake of Mongolia's transition to democracy and closer US-Mongolia relations, China's relationship with Mongolia has become more complicated. China regards the deepening ties between the two countries as evidence of a US plan to contain China. The elevation of Mongolia's importance to the US, marked by Bush's visit, has caused some in Beijing to reevaluate and seek to adjust their relationship with Mongolia. In 2005, China and Mongolia issued a joint-statement, agreeing that neither would engage in an alliance that would negatively affect the other's interests, implying Mongolia's relationship with the United States was threatening to China's interest.[226] The US has good reason to strengthen its relationship with Mongolia,

224.Wang, "(2006).

225.Alan M. Wachman, "Suffering What it Must? Mongolia and the Power of the Weak," Orbis: Vol. 54, No. 4 (2010).

226. Wang, (2006).

emphasize common values and provide support that further entrenches Mongolian democracy. However, the US will have to reassure China that deepening US-Mongolia ties are not counter to China's interests and actively seek ways to establish trilateral coordination.

.....

-IV-

Yunnan's Relation with Vietnam and Myanmar

"All ethnic minorities are important members of the Chinese family," Hu said.

Remarks made by Hu Jintao on an inspection of Yunnan, July 2009.

A Sino-Vietnam friendship sign at the border market in Jinping County, Yunnan[227]

227. Author's photo.

Geography and Topography

Yunnan Province occupies 390,000 sq. km of the southwest corner of China, home to China's most ethnically diverse population totaling 45 million, including 14 million minorities from 14 groups. 94% of Yunnan terrain is mountainous, epitomizing the proverb used for centuries to explain the difficulties of governing the far reaches of the empire - the mountains are high and the emperor is far away. China's leaders throughout history have largely ignored Yunnan, contributing to its isolation and a local sense of independence, fostered as much by mountains as invasions by both Burmese and Northern Chinese dynasties. Even today, Yunnan culture is shaped by the descendants of Ming, Qing and Nationalist armies that had fought in the region and settled there after hostilities ended, keeping their diverse cultures and religions even to this day. Today, however, the Central government pays greater attention to Yunnan compared to predecessors. This is partly a result of the government's recognition of the geostrategic importance of border areas, partly because of greater political interconnectedness between the provinces and the center compared to historic governance structures, as well as the national drive to modernize the country.

Yunnan is a landlocked province, like Jilin and Inner Mongolia, making its land borders with neighboring states the locus for international commerce. Yunnan shares 4,060 kilometers of international borders with Vietnam to the Southeast, Laos to the South and Myanmar, its longest border at 2,000 kilometers to the West. Yunnan's neighboring provinces and autonomous regions include Sichuan, Guizhou, Guangxi and Tibet. Its geostrategic location between the Chinese heartland, the Himalayas and Southeast Asia have historically made Yunnan a crossroads between diverse Asian cultures, though forbidding terrain (jungles to the South and mountains to the North and West) and relatively underdeveloped kingdoms in neighboring states ensured throughout history that it never enjoyed the prosperity of seaports on China's East coast or trading posts along the Silk Routes to Central Asia. Assuredly, it remains a cross-road today and its leaders seek to capitalize on its geographic advantages to promote economic growth and social stability while simultaneously tackling contemporary non-traditional transnational security threats including human and drug trafficking and infectious diseases.

In the 2nd century BC during the Han Dynasty, Chinese forces invaded modern day Yunnan and assimilated it into China. Despite this martial integration, the region retained much of its independence and functioned as a vassal state to the dominant Chinese empire for more than a thousand years. During this period, the region was ruled by different ethnically-based kingdoms such the Nanzhao in the Tang Dynasty and the Dali during the Song. It was not until the Yuan Dynasty in the 13th century that direct control was exercised over the region following the Mongol leader Kublai Khan's conquests. However even as an official province of China, the area enjoyed significant autonomy due to the emperor's inability to exercise effective authority that could stretch to the far reaches of the empire's domain. During the Yuan and Ming Dynasties, local chieftains held significant power much as they did in prior periods, though they paid formal taxes to the central government rather than occasional tribute. In the Qing Dynasty, the area fell further under the central government's control, though local authority was still largely dominated by ethnic groups. During the Republican period, particularly during the Anti-Japanese War (as the Chinese parochially refer to World War II), Han Chinese migration to Yunnan increased rapidly as the Manchuria and coastal provinces were occupied by Japanese forces and Yunnan became a base for Nationalist resistance. Yunnan and its capitol, Kunming became a critical logistics hub for war material supplied by the United States by air to their

Chinese allies. American volunteer pilots comprising the "American Volunteer Group," more famously known as the Flying Tigers, flew out of airfields in Yunnan. Following the attack on Pearl Harbor in December 1941, the Flying Tigers and other American units formally became part of the U.S. Army.

Yunnan's geostrategic importance was underscored after the Japanese invasion of the then-British colony of Burma cutting off land-routes used to supply American and Chinese forces with war materials. Supplies were airlifted from British India over the Himalayas to airfields in Yunnan, a route American pilots dubbed, "the Hump." By 1943, U.S. and allied forces led by Sinophile General Joseph Stillwell fought the Japanese in the jungles of Burma and re-opened the land route from Ledo, India to Kunming. Today where the "Stillwell road" as it is called crosses over a stream demarking the border between China and Myanmar at the town of Wanding, the wrought iron bridge made in Illinois and installed by an African-American U.S. Army engineering unit stands as a testimony to U.S.-China cooperation.

Yunnan is a reminder of China's diversity; both in terms of ethnic and cultural differences as well as the economic disparity between urban and rural areas, and coastal and hinterland provinces. About 26 ethnic minorities are officially recognized in province, though numerous other communities are considered ethnically diverse but are not recognized by the government because they have fewer than 5,000 people. This is the greatest ethnic diversity found in a single Chinese province, where about half of China's 56 ethnic groups account for 38% of the province's population. The largest ethnic groups in Yunnan are the Yi, Bai, Dai, Naxi, Hani and Zhuang. These groups also inhabit the border areas and their members reside on both sides of the national boundary.[228]

---

228. ", People's Government of Yunnan Province, August 25, 2005. Accessed at: http://www.yn.gov.cn/yunnan,china/77405618595430400/20050825/522006.html

Financial Investment in Infrastructure, PBWM

In Yunnan and the rest of China, the last decade's economic growth was driven by the State' investment in fixed assets and infrastructure. Yunnan's fixed asset investments have grown dramatically province-wide, while particular effort has been made to channel investment to border regions. In 1995, Yunnan logged $398 million in State fixed asset investments. That figure jumped to $7 billion in 2000, increasing to $12 billion in 2005 and reaching $18 billion in 2007. Border counties and prefectures were significant recipients of these resources. Honghe Prefecture, which includes Hekou city on the Vietnam border had $2 billion in investment in 2007, about half as much as the provincial capital, Kunming and more than any other sub-provincial jurisdiction. In 2008, the province branded its development plan, the "Bridgehead Strategy," describing its infrastructure investments as part of a comprehensive blueprint to position the province to take advantage of its proximity to resource-rich Myanmar and Northern Vietnam.[229]

In July 2009, President Hu Jintao made an inspection tour of Yunnan province, declaring that the province was now a "bridgehead" for China's relations with Southeast and South Asia. Investments in infrastructure linking Yunnan to the rest of Asia is at the core of this new "bridgehead strategy," as Chinese officials in the province seek to link it to neighbor states and capitalize on the central government's foreign policy objectives and key achievements like the China-ASEAN Free Trade Agreement which came into effect in 2009, reducing tariffs on thousands of widely products. Yunnan's proximity to geostrategically important Southeast Asian nations makes it an important focal point for infrastructure investments.

229. 2008 Yunnan Provincial Statistical Yearbook.

High profile projects include oil and gas pipelines built by China National Petroleum Company (CNPC), running from Myanmar's Kyaukpyu port to Kunming. The pipelines will enable China to access Myanmar's energy resources and provide a land-bridge for oil from the Middle East to reach western China, bypassing the narrow Straits of Malacca that some Chinese strategists fear could be a choke point should the U.S. or other naval power seek to cut off China's energy supply. The pipelines will thread their way across Myanmar, crossing the border at Ruili in Yunnan, continuing to Kunming where refineries and a distribution network will provide energy for Yunnan's economic development. The natural gas pipeline will continue on from Kunming to Guangxi and Guizhou provinces further diversifying Southwest China's energy supply and reducing strain on transport infrastructure between China's ports and less developed inland provinces. Other major investments include a railway running the same route as the pipeline and a major railway station, which will connect Yunnan to Southeast Asian rail networks, including the 100-year old Kunming-Hanoi line built by the French. To cement its status as the center of the bridgehead strategy, the province is planning to build a new, $3 billion international airport in Kunming (the current one dates back to 1923). Tentatively named after Kunming native Zheng He, the Ming Dynasty admiral who led voyages to Southeast Asia and Africa in the early 15th century.[230]

230."The Fourth Air Hub in China - Kunming International New Airport," Yunnan Airport Group Website, accessed at: http://www.ynairport.com/infoPublish/news.do?func=issue&action=staticInfo&type=topic&language=en See also, "New Kunming Airport to name Zheng He International Airport," Kunming City Government Information Portal, Februrary 9, 2009. Accessed at: http://en.kunming.cn/index/content/2009-02/09/content_1745058.htm

Yunnan's large cities, including its capital Kunming are developmentally on par with other provincial capitals, boasting skyscrapers, new roads and highways without potholes and massive airports and bridges that characterize China's investment driven growth model. Cities like Hekou in Honghe prefecture are connected to Kunming by four-lane divided concrete highways while rail lines are under construction and other highways are currently being carved through the mountains until they eventually reach other border crossings, including Jinping County with Vietnam. However, the province remains poor compared to China's east coast and is largely underdeveloped. Dehong prefecture and its border crossings at Ruili and Wanding lack the highway and rail links that contribute to Hekou's prosperity. Three quarters of Yunnan's population still live in rural areas where incomes lag far behind cities. In 2007, farmers' average annual income in Yunnan stood at just RMB2,634 or less than USD420 (at RMB6.3:1).[231]

To address these imbalances, the government has launched ambitious anti-poverty campaigns which channel government resources and investment to the poorest parts of the province, many of which are in border regions. As in the other provinces in this report, the most comprehensive of these programs is the PBWM project. In 2005, eight of Yunnan's prefectures and municipalities were enrolled in the program, establishing projects in 25 counties. Investments have focused on infrastructure, including building the rural road network, electrification, drinking water and waste water treatment, rural irrigation, forestry/animal husbandry and traditional medicines, public health, and education amongst many other areas. In particular, investments have been made in building border infrastructure, particularly in constructing facilities to facilitate larger-scale border crossing, including inspection stations and information

231. 2008 Yunnan Provincial Statistical Yearbook.

networks that enable larger numbers of citizens from each side of the border to cross daily to trade in government-invested markets. Progress in this area is easily measured. As of 2008, only 75 of the province's 12,798 administrative villages remained without electricity, while 185 were not served by a paved road.[232] However, despite these massive investments, poverty remains entrenched in many parts of the province, with more than 5.55 million people classified as impoverished according to national poverty standards.

From 2005 to 2007, during the first phase of the PBWM project in Yunnan, 540 million RMB was invested by all levels of government. From 2008 to 2009, 1.54 billion RMB was invested, including 130 million from the Ministry of Finance and National Development and Reform Commission, 1 billion from other departments and 402 million from prefectures and municipalities under the province. Border regions have absorbed investment to improve housing for residents, access to public utilities, education, power and transport networks. Funds have been used to promote cash crops, including herbs and plants used in traditional medicine.[233]

In February 2008, a delegation of central government officials representing 23 ministries, commissions and agencies visited Yunnan on an inspection of PBWM programs. The State Council subsequently issued a document, referred to as "recommendations" that was interpreted as an endorsement of provincial efforts, resulting in the Central government committing to invest a further RMB150 million in Yunnan's border areas over the next three years. However, past investments have not brought prosperity to all citizens. In the 25 counties on Yunnan's international borders, the average income of farmers is 2,273 RMB, 47% of the national average.

---

232. 2008 Yunnan Statistical Yearbook.

233. Interviews in Yunnan Province, June 2010.

Yunnan's gains in reducing poverty and promoting economic and social development through investment are tenuous, raising concerns about sustainability amongst provincial leaders. Urbanization has been slow in Yunnan, with no city in the province other than the capital with a population of over 500,000.[234] Despite having about 3.4% of the country's population, the province only contributes 1.9% of the country's GDP. In 1995, the province ranked 18th in GDP, falling to 23 in 2001 and 24 in 2009. Average incomes in the province are half the national average, ranking the province 29 out of 31. Of 129 counties in the province, 80 are designated as impoverished -- the highest number in the nation. Interestingly, only 73 counties are recognized by the central government as impoverished, an indication of the politics of poverty where the province seeks to pressure the central government for greater allocations of assistance. Both the central government and local government set standards for poverty, often creating statistical discrepancies, exaggerated by the contradictory incentives for local-level officials seeking to report accomplishments in poverty reduction to higher level officials, while simultaneously emphasizing the scope of the problem in order to secure additional aid from the central government and external donors.

Yunnan's mountainous terrain is one explanation for the province's relative poverty. Arable land is limited. One county on Yunnan's border with Vietnam is called Jinping, which literally means "gold-level." A local official explained that the name derives from scarcity of level ground in the mountains the massive labor investment required over centuries to turn the mountainsides into terraced fields

234. According to 2000 census figures. Yunnan's second largest city is Quiing with a population of about 311,000.

makes the flat pieces of land as valuable as gold.[235] Over 600 rivers flow throughout the province, including the Yangtze, Mekong, and Pearl Rivers. These rivers and drops in elevation generate substantial amounts of hydro-energy, enough to provide every person in the province with four times the national average of energy from hydropower, though officials state that the potential resources have not been adequately exploited yet. Yunnan's four major industries are tobacco, biotech, mining, and tourism. The province is rich in natural resources and boasts the largest deposits of aluminum, lead, tin, and zinc in the country as well as significant amounts of copper, nickel, coal and iron. In many parts of the country, prosperity is centered on mines and tobacco factories. The border regions which lack these natural resources and advantageous topography can only look to neighboring states and their geographic location for competitive advantage. Despite the massive investments that have been made to date, local officials identify the need for more investment in border facilities, including crossing points, transport infrastructure, border trade development zones and other infrastructure to promote trans-border economic development.

Poverty, Transnational Non-Traditional Security Threats

Despite natural resources, pervasive poverty in many areas indicates that Yunnan faces significant challenges to the province's development strategies. Transnational criminal networks foster corruption. Heroin and synthetic narcotics produced in Myanmar and the Golden Triangle are smuggled through Yunnan in large quantities. Traffickers use historic trade routes, including the "Stilwell Road" and modern transport means to move narcotics to Kunming, then on to other major consuming markets in China. China

235.Local guidebooks also claim the name derives from the Jin and Ping Rivers which merge at Jinping.

has historically been a transit point for Burmese heroin exported abroad, explaining why high grade heroin in the U.S. and Europe was called "China white." Today, high grade heroin is readily found in Yunnan and drug addicts from other cities travel to cities closer to the border to buy and use high grade drugs before they are adulterated by traffickers farther along their distribution routes. While Yunnan was never considered an important destination for drugs, which were largely bound for major markets in the U.S. and Europe (though increasing affluence in China's cities have made them more important markets in their own right) traffickers have sought to develop markets all along their transit routes as a means to finance their logistics. Essentially, narcotics wholesalers determined that they could generate retail-level profits along their routes. Yunnan, which has a long history of poppy cultivation and opium consumption in its own right during the Qing and Republican periods, became a major drug using province following reform and opening period in 1978. As everywhere else in the world, drug addiction in Yunnan brought with it misery and poverty which hampers its development to this day.

Unsurprisingly, the first indigenous case of HIV/AIDS was detected in the largest border crossing with Myanmar at Ruili City in 1989. In 1999, Yunnan made up almost half of all HIV-positive cases in the country, although that figure fell to 32% by 2002 as increased testing and surveillance throughout the country revealed that the disease was present in virtually every province, including a large-scale epidemic in Henan province caused by unsanitary blood and plasma collection practices rather than intravenous drug use. In 2003, China began a national HIV/AIDS treatment program, providing free anti-retroviral drugs and other services to infected people. National and internationally funded public health programs, including bilateral aid from England and America supplemented national and provincial budgets to address not only the ravages of HIV/AIDS, but other public health challenges including malaria. Unfortunately, because of poor governance and the lack of public health services on the Myanmar-side of the border, Yunnan has little chance of overcoming many of the challenges that will continue to cross national boundaries. On the portion of the Yunnan border with Vietnam, similar though smaller-scale cross border public health challenges arise from emerging infectious diseases in animal populations and cross-border networks of drug dealers, addicts and sex workers who lack access to public health services and education. Reservoir populations of unchecked and untreated HIV/AIDS, malaria, tuberculosis, influenza will mitigate achievements that are made on the Chinese-side of the border.

The central, provincial and locals governments on the border are not passive actors and have several programs to address cross border challenges. While the central and provincial governments provide resources and an enabling policy environment, local-level officials implement plans and strategies that extend their influence across the national boundary. Cross-border programs have addressed public health issues, like HIV/AIDS and in particular, counter-narcotics operations in Myanmar. In 2003, various government and international agencies estimated that between 80 and 2,300 tons of heroin were trafficked from Myanmar to China, though more recent estimates place the total production in the golden triangle closer to 400 tons. In 2004, China began expanding its counter-narcotics efforts, announcing a "People's War against Drugs" in April 2005. National budgets for fighting drugs were increased and new compulsory rehab and detoxification facilities were built and staffed by officers under the Public Security ministry while public health authorities began establishing methadone clinics. In addition to these demand-side interventions, a program to interdict supplies of opium and heroin from Myanmar was initiated. Recognizing that the problem was not limited to Myanmar, China and Vietnam's public security ministers signed an MOU in 2006, agreeing to, "Take measures to crack down on terrorism, women and children trafficking, illegal border crossings, drugs trafficking and money counterfeiting, and cult organization and instigation."[236]

In 2006, the Chinese government formally announced the existence of a poppy-substitution program that it had been operating in Myanmar, revealing in 2008 that it had spent 700 million RMB on the program.[237] Similar programs had been implemented since the mid-1990s to work with Burmese poppy farmers to entice and cajole them to give up growing poppy flowers and cultivate other cash crops, such as tobacco, tea and rubber. These programs often met with limited success or were otherwise unsustainable due to the lack of profitable crop substitutes, though significant success can be attributed to more recent programs. However, China's approach to designing and implementing cross-border programs has been consistent over time and relied on careful coordination and consensus-building with counterparts in Myanmar. Chinese authorities also worked closely with the United Nations Office of Drugs and Crime (UNODC), which added to the program's air of legitimacy and likely contributed to promoting greater trust building with the Myanmar government and ethnic groups controlling different areas along China's border. China's stated foreign policy principle of not interfering in the affairs of other states is closely observed in this intervention model, where government and non-government stakeholder buy in is considered crucial by the Chinese-side.

---

236. "China, Vietnam Strengthen Joint Crackdown on Border Crimes," Xinhua, May 12, 2006.
237. "China gives Myanmar $100m for poppy eradication," AFP, June 26, 2008.

To some extent, this explains the periods of failure and success for crop-substitution attempts. During periods when the Myanmar government or ethnic group was willing to stop poppy cultivation, the program succeeded. Some critics of the program have claimed that Chinese merchants have bullied Burmese farmers into buying Chinese seeds and fertilizer, while also complaining that dependence on the Chinese market alone for crops depresses prices. Complaints about implementation on the Myanmar-side of the border, including financial abuses, overuse of chemical pesticides and fertilizers and a lack of farmers' participation in design of the program have resulted in crop failures and bankruptcy for many rural Burmese. Nonetheless, the relative success of the program measured by reduced poppy cultivation however reveals that in this case, China does not exercise coercive influence over authorities in neighboring areas, even when confronting a non-traditional security threat that directly threatened Chinese interests on Chinese soil.

Local authorities in Yunnan's Ruili have taken an innovative approach to implementing crop-substitution programs in Myanmar. Rather than taking a purely government-to-government approach (which would have been straightforward since Naypyitaw controls the territory in that part of the border), the Ruili authorities enrolled local companies to play a critical role in implementing the project. The Ruili government provided funds to companies involved in various sectors, including infrastructure and agriculture, sending them across the border to work with local government leaders and farmers to encourage them to begin cultivating cash crops that those companies would purchase and ship to China. The local government provided duty-free status to these products and exempted them from import licensing requirements that apply to many food items imported into China. By 2007, 135 companies were involved in the program.[238] With China's relative increase in wealth, rising prices and growing demand for food, the program crop-substitution became economically more viable and potentially more stable. By many accounts, the supply of heroin from Myanmar has been greatly reduced since 2006, though statistics are contradictory and often unreliable. Ultimately however, the success of the program and amount of drugs being produced in Myanmar and trafficked to China are more likely dependent on developments within Myanmar, particularly the re-emerging conflict between Naypiytaw and ethnic groups along the border following the 2010 elections.

The scourge of drugs originating in the Golden Triangle region has created an HIV/AIDS epidemic in the border region. In 2009 Yunnan official statistics identified 3,193 HIV-infected persons in its 25 border counties, making up 25% of the province's total. Though the province's total number of estimated cases reached 80,000 in 2004, provincial officials consider the border region to be the front lines of the battle against the disease.[239] Yunnan's HIV/AIDS challenges are both indigenous as well as transnational, particularly because of large populations of infected persons across its borders. Myanmar's problem is particularly serious, with an estimated 360,000 cases and a national prevalence rate of 1.3% in 2005.[240] By comparison, Vietnam has an estimated 260,000 cases, though its national prevalence rate is about

238. "Report on China's participation in GMS cooperation released," Xinhua, March 28, 2008.
239. Yan Xiao, Sibylle Kristensen, Jiangping Sun, Lin Lu, and Sten H. Vermund,
"Expansion of HIV/AIDS in China: Lessons from Yunnan Province," Soc Sci Med. 2007 February; 64(3): 665–675.
240. Yunnan Province HIV/AIDS Work Report, 2010.

half a percent.[241]

Yunnan's HIV/AIDS programs have been heavily under written by financial support from the Central government and international aid agencies, such as the UK's DFID, USAID, AUSAID, the Global Fund Against AIDS, Tuberculosis and Malaria (GFATM), and numerous private programs implemented by non-government organizations. Yunnan is considered a particularly tolerant location for foreign NGOs. National programs, including the PBWM program have dedicated HIV/AIDS projects, building government capacity in the 25 border counties and addressing the government's top priorities including prevention education and expanded testing. The program built 232 HIV testing centers which conducted 450,000 tests over the course of 2009, accounting for a fifth of all tests conducted in the province. The province also established programs to provide treatment and care for HIV-positive patients and raise awareness amongst officials down to village-level cadres and amongst officials in towns with border-crossings.

The PBWM program in Yunnan also provided the resources and framework for the province's "People's War against Drugs and AIDS," which is entering its final year in 2010. The province enacted programs to encourage condom use and clean needles amongst vulnerable groups including cross-border long-distance truck drivers and injecting drug users. Prevention education activities were conducted in towns and villages along the border and health checks were conducted for frequent border crossers. In border counties,

---

241."Vietnam HIV/AIDS Estimates and Projections 2007 - 2012," UNAIDS, 2009.
Accessed at:
http://www.unaids.org.vn/sitee/images/stories/EPP%20report%20EN.pdf

education programs were established for the People's Armed Police units guarding crossings, health inspectors and foreign affairs officers.

Recognizing that effectively controlling the disease would require interventions on both sides of the border, Yunnan officials have participated in a regional HIV/AIDS program funded by the Australian aid agency, AUSAID. Established in 2008 and running through 2012, the program aims to reduce HIV spread through injecting drugs, supporting interventions such as clean needle exchange, methadone and behavior change programs. Furthermore, the program creates a cross-border cooperation infrastructure that enables Yunnan (and Guangxi, the other program site), to more effectively engage their counterparts with Vietnam, Laos and Myanmar. Focusing on three ports with Myanmar; Ruili-Muse, Longchuan-Rigang, Nabang- Laisa and one with Vietnam; Hekou-Lao Cai, the project underwrites annual and biannual meetings between local officials from each side, putting counterparts at different levels and with different functions at face-to-face meetings to discuss HIV/AIDS programs and interventions. This includes cross-border training and technical exchange, monitoring and evaluation of programs and research on new infections occurring on both sides of the border amongst injecting drug users.

Like narcotics, public health challenges particularly HIV/AIDS has spurred cross-border cooperation between Yunnan security forces and their counterparts in neighboring states. AUSAID funded the establishment of the "Yunnan Risk Reduction Study Center" at the Yunnan Police Academy in Puning County. At the center, police officers from Myanmar, Laos and Vietnam meet with Chinese counterparts and receive training and exchange information. Yunnan's police force China's most experienced in dealing with heroin abuse and HIV/AIDS and has therefore taken responsibility for training its own officers and those from other provinces to increase their understanding of the causes and effects of HIV/AIDS, how to reduce workplace exposure and reduce the spread of the virus to officers. In 2005 and 2006, UNAIDS supported Yunnan's efforts to train police in Myanmar, laying the foundation for more ambitious cross-border programs funded by AUSAID and Chinese government sources.[242] Yunnan province's efforts to address trans-boundary threats are an important component of its overall "Bridgehead" strategy towards Southeast Asia and its bordering states.

China's Geostrategic View of Myanmar and Vietnam

Myanmar and Vietnam, like North Korea and Mongolia are seen though both a geo-strategic and local lens when viewed from Beijing. Both Vietnam and Myanmar are vitally important to Yunnan's strategy for economic development. In addition to economic opportunities, however, Myanmar and Vietnam both present challenges at both national and local levels.

Myanmar

The Myanmar-China relationship is complex, due to both contemporary political issues as well as historic anxiety that characterizes the asymmetrical relationship that China has with smaller states on its border. Predictably, Myanmar recognizes China's size and influence, though remains wary of becoming overly dependent or otherwise dominated by China. These fears are exacerbated by China's economic dominance, as well as China's global influence and Myanmar's isolation. Myanmar has been careful to avoid becoming a virtual vassal state, balancing its relations with China against India and ASEAN nations.

China's strategic view of Myanmar is similarly

242. Authors' interviews.

sophisticated. China's recognizes Myanmar's geostrategic advantages, acting to leverage them through strategic investment such as the oil and gas pipelines and Chinese-funded infrastructure projects in Myanmar including the port at Sitwe. While some analysts and journalists have likely exaggerated China's influence and ability to project power into the Indian Ocean through Myanmar, there is little doubt that Beijing is carefully cultivating its relations with Naypyitaw as part of a broader strategy to become a regional or global power.

Despite Chinese aspirations, Myanmar remains an independent state with a strong sense of identity and nationalism and a history of resisting foreign influences, though the numerous domestic challenges that complicate Beijing's Myanmar strategy present require careful management at the local and national levels. Border security is a key concern for the bilateral relationship and one that requires the close coordination between central government officials and Yunnan. The Chinese ministry of defense revealed that the PLA "took over" defense of the Yunnan section of the China-Myanmar border in 2003, relieving the People's Armed Police from their customary responsibility. In 2004 the two militaries signed an MOU on border defense, establishing a bilateral talks mechanism and increasing bilateral cooperation on managing the border and addressing cross border crime.[243]

Border security has been a significant concern for Chinese authorities, particularly following the escalation of tensions between the Myanmar government and ethnic groups in the border region prior to the 2010 elections. Those tensions culminated in an armed clash in August 2009 between the government and the leaders of the Kokang district

243."China, Myanmar Sign MOU on Border Defense," Xinhua, December 5, 2004.

adjacent to Yunnan. When the Kokang army was routed by troops commanded by Naypyitaw, 37,000 refugees, mostly ethnic Chinese residents of Kokang district fled to safety in Yunnan. Chinese officials demarched their Myanmar counterparts, urging them to "properly handle domestic problems and maintain stability in the China-Myanmar border region."[244] Exactly a year later, General Than Shwe, the chairman of Myanmar's State Peace and Development Council visited Beijing on the eve of Myanmar's elections which coincided with the 60th anniversary of China-Myanmar relations. According to the Chinese Foreign Ministry's statement following the summit with Hu Jintao, concerns about border security remain acute. Hu called on both sides to jointly safeguard peace and stability of the frontier and boost economic and social development of the border areas: "China respects sovereignty and territorial integrity of Myanmar, understands and supports the Myanmar government's efforts for national reconciliation." He vowed to enhance cooperation with Myanmar in border management and intensify efforts to jointly combat cross border crimes for sound production and life order of the border regions.[245]

Managing security on the border remains a challenge, however, particularly due to weak governance and capacity on the Myanmar side. Civilian officials in a border county in Yunnan highlighted that while the border remains open and relatively secure, there is little they can do to accelerate economic development or deepen their local-level relations.

---

244. Tim Johnston, "China Urges Burma to Bridle Ethnic Militia Uprising at Border," Washington Post, August 29, 2009.

245. "Hu Jintao Holds Talks with Chairman of Myanmar's State Peace and Development Council Than Shwe," Ministry of Foreign Affairs, the People's Republic of China, September 9, 2010.

They highlighted that regular interactions with Myanmar counterparts are maintained, facilitated by regular meetings of "border committees" that are legitimized by MOUs signed at the national level. Cross-border official contacts are both formal and informal, involving officials from Dehong Prefecture and cities and counties along the border. Chinese officials in one border town invite their Myanmar counterparts to an annual banquet once a year, while officials responsible for trade, security and foreign affairs meet with their Myanmar counterparts regularly, sometimes as often as twice a week for a county foreign affairs officer. The framework of bilateral interactions at the central, provincial and prefecture levels creates the legal and policy framework that enables local officials on both sides to agree to reciprocal policies requiring frequent local coordination to manage the border, such as issuing border passes to local residents and repatriating citizens accused of crimes.

Cross-border trade and investment is a significant aspect of the local-level relationship between China and Myanmar. Chinese outbound investment has been growing rapidly, and investors from Yunnan are active throughout the country, but particularly in the border areas. Commercial and foreign affairs officers on the Chinese side seek to create the right conditions to attract trade from Myanmar to their individual border crossings, providing covered markets and ensuring that entry/exit formalities are relatively quick.

However, officials in Yunnan's border area express concern about their Myanmar counterparts' lack of capacity that is reflected in their inability to provide services to their citizens. One Chinese expert pointed out the inadequacy of the health system was reflected in the numbers of Myanmar officials who travel to Kunming to seek medical care. Addressing cross-border infectious disease has proven difficult, as has dealing with other cross-border threats such as drug trafficking. One Chinese official speculated that a challenge on the Myanmar side was the lack of coordination between the capital in Naypyitaw and officials in border regions. Yunnan authorities' jobs are complicated in that some areas along the border are controlled by the central government, while some are under the control of autonomous ethnic groups. Further complicating matters is the lack of close coordination between civil and military authorities on both sides of the border. One Chinese official lamented that when faced with a problem in Myanmar, often, "there is no one to talk to."[246]

The lack of a functioning legal system, particularly in the border areas creates management challenges for Chinese bureaucrats who are frequently drawn into commercial disputes between Chinese and Myanmar parties. Growing investment and trade has increased the number of disputes and increased officials' workloads. To encourage more commerce, Chinese authorities initiated discussions with their Myanmar counterparts in 2006 to expand the use of RMB for transactions on the Myanmar side of the border, but one Chinese official stated that its use had not become common-place and that RMB could only be used in border towns, not further inland such as the regional hub of Lashio. By 2009, cross-border trade at the port of Ruili and Jiegao in Dehong Prefecture accounted for more than half of Yunnan's and almost a third of the country's trade with Myanmar, amounting to RMB 56.87 billion. However, because of the challenges of operating in Myanmar and growing numbers of disputes, local officials in Ruili claimed they were no longer encouraging Chinese companies to invest in Myanmar and that they had opened an office address disputes with Myanmar trade officials.

Those economic opportunities are tempered by the non-

246. Authors' interview, Yunnan, June 2010.

traditional security threats that loosely governed Myanmar presents. The border police report that about a third of the robberies in Ruili are committed by foreigners and that they face major problems with illegal border crossings, smuggling, illegal overstayers and migrants illegally employed on the Chinese side. To coordinate security with counterparts, the PLA and People's Armed Police Border Guards meet formally with their Myanmar counterparts every two weeks while Public Security authorities meet monthly. With 20,000 daily crossings, 90% of whom are local residents, the security authorities have established specialized tasks and units to deal with the complexities of multi-ethnic and multi-national challenges. The Ruili police have UN-trained officers in a department dedicated to trafficking, responsible for tracking down and repatriating trafficked women and children back to Myanmar. To better understand local culture and languages, People's Armed Police border guard units, which include officers from all over China, ensure that 5 to 8 percent of their force include local minority members. To address drug trafficking, Ruili has two police dog breeding and training bases, one for the border guards and one for Customs. Because Ruili is a major smuggling point as well as the top border crossing between China and Myanmar, police departments in other parts of China post liaison officers there to coordinate investigations and assist with the extradition of criminals caught elsewhere in China.

Vietnam

Compared to Dehong Prefecture along the Myanmar border, Honghe Prefecture shares similar traits including geography, ethnic minority groups straddling the border and a common strategy to leverage border trade and infrastructure to drive economic growth in China. However, China's relationship with Vietnam is characterized by greater mutual mistrust than with Myanmar, driven partly by the unresolved maritime border, but also because of lingering resentment over the 1979 border war. While mistrust and history have not hindered trade on the Vietnam-China border any more than it has between former belligerents throughout Northeast Asia, the Vietnamese government's coherency and capacity reduces transnational security threats and enables the Vietnamese to take greater advantage of the economic opportunities that China presents when compared to the other border areas in this study.

At the national level, China-Vietnam relations are marked by a degree of distrust, fed by both a history of colonization and contemporary conflict, but also by Vietnamese concerns about economic dominance by its much larger neighbor. China's military modernization has also prompted Vietnam to increase its defense spending and acquire submarines and fighter planes from Russia. Chinese assertiveness over its sovereignty over the South China Sea, including disputed islands and undersea resources has lead Vietnam to strengthen its relationship with the United States, fueling mistrust on China's part.

China actively has sought to defuse tensions with Vietnam and erase the memories of the brutal 1979 border war. Bilateral ties began improving following the collapse of the Soviet Union and Vietnam's withdrawal from Cambodia, normalizing diplomatic relations in 1991. A landmine clearing campaign China's border area began in 1992 and lasting two years, followed by a second round in 1997, with the clearing work largely completed by 2008. A joint committee was formed in 2001 to begin marking the border, and by early 2009, it had been completely demarcated. With the hardest of security threats at the border resolved, greater space was created for the two sides to begin to engage in further confidence building measures and trade.

Vietnam's economic reforms, known as doi moi, contribute to improving China-Vietnam ties due to pragmatic foreign policies and growing trade. As labor and material costs increase in China, Vietnam becomes an increasingly attractive destination for investment. Chinese companies, including many from Yunnan invest in and do business with Vietnam. The relatively strong capacity of the Vietnamese government is reflected in a safe investment environment and regular interactions between local-level officials from both sides of the border. That said, economic development is uneven in different parts of the border. For instance, two different border crossings in Honghe Prefecture; Jinping and Hekou have markedly different levels of economic activity, despite similar strategies to boost cross-border trade.

Jinping County

Jinping County is designated as an impoverished area, eligible for subsidies and poverty alleviation support from various levels of government. In addition to financial resources, the central government appoints senior officials from the Foreign Ministry to serve for fixed terms (about two years) in Jinping to both increase Jinping's human capacity and give central government officials experience working in impoverished regions.

Like other border crossings on China's periphery, Jinping County has built border markets, allows for small-scale duty free trade and permits citizens in the border region to travel freely between the two countries. At the Jinshuihe border crossing, local authorities are planning to develop a sprawling industrial zone near the border market. However, due to several factors, trade is small scale and disappoints local authorities, though they are optimistic that they can eventually develop sustainable trade. The local commerce bureau subsidizes a customs broker to maintain an office at the border market, providing free rent and computers. They also subsidize the participation of Chinese business people to attend Vietnamese trade fairs. However, poverty persists on both sides of the border, limiting the prospect for large-scale commercial transactions. Furthermore, the chief agricultural product grown in the mountainous fields on the Vietnamese-side are sweet potatoes which cannot be brought into China without a difficult to obtain import license. One official lamented that the inability to buy Vietnamese sweet potatoes limits the amount of cash on the Vietnamese-side of the border, reducing the possibility of Vietnamese farmers coming to the border market to buy Chinese goods.

The Jinping government expressed frustration with their inability to directly lobby Beijing to increase quotas and loosen the license restrictions on importing staple foods from Vietnam. However, they have sought other means to build trade. Jinping County has promoted local companies to "go abroad" and invest in Vietnam, with three Jinping based companies having opened offices in northern Vietnam. To support them and encourage more investment, the Jinping government has opened a liaison office in Dianbian city in Vietnam, the closest major city on the highway leading from Jinping. However, despite the Jinping government's promotion of trade and investment, the Jinshuihe bridge at the Vietnam border is quiet most days with few trucks or pedestrians crossing, except on holidays when local farmers cross to visit family and buy or sell vegetables. Commercial-scale transactions remain elusive despite the infrastructure built on the Chinese-side of the border.

Hekou City

Compared to Jinping County, Hekou is in an advantageous position to capitalize on economic growth in China and Vietnam's reform and opening. While Jinping straddles the highway to Dianbian, Hekou is strategically located at the border crossing of the century-old Hanoi Kunming railway. With major highways extending from Hekou North to Kunming and South to Hanoi, it is a major transit point for cargo and passengers. Hekou was a major supply depot and crossing point for war materiel used by North Vietnam during the conflict with America (and by China during the 1979 war),, bestowing the city with infrastructure not present at other border crossings.

Hekou's border markets are vibrant, hosting both small scale transactions as well as commercial scale ones. The bridge separating Hekou and Lao Cai on the Vietnamese side is thronged with border citizens crossing to market, and it is one of the few border crossings where third-country citizens are allowed to cross. At 8am each morning when the customs offices open on each side, up to 10,000 Vietnamese rush across the bridge to line up at inspection stations on the Chinese side before setting up their wares in the border markets in Hekou. Clutching border passes, the Vietnamese traders crossing on foot are followed by bicycles and trucks with larger consignments of Vietnamese goods being exported to China. Unlike other border crossings, Lao Cai appears to have taken full advantage of its proximity to the border and China's expanding economy. High-rise buildings and apartment blocks mark Lao Cai's skyline.

Hekou officials indicate that growing wealth on both sides of the border have contributed to greater appreciation for the benefits of a positive bilateral relationship. Separated by the narrow Honghe River marking the border, residents of Hekou said that they could not approach the border in the 1980s without being harassed by sniper fire from the Vietnamese-side. Today, children swim in the river and cavort on the banks with out raising an eyebrow. This positive political and economic environment is underpinned by regular interactions between civilian officials and confidence building measures between security forces from both sides.. In and around Hekou, Chinese and Vietnamese security forces including border guard detachments conduct joint patrols of the border area. One Chinese official described joint patrols often ending with banquets and revelry by officers from both sides taking part. Civilian officials claim that they have multiple meetings per week with their counterparts on the Vietnamese side, in addition to regularly scheduled official meetings that form the framework of the bilateral relationship at the local level.

National-level treaties between Beijing and Hanoi include clauses that permit such local-level interactions in the context of bilateral relations, prompting one local official to joke, "My work is just a clause in the big MOU!"[247]

Implications for U.S. Interests

China's relations with Vietnam and Myanmar have both high-level, strategic importance and local implications as well. China's multi-tiered management of their relations with Myanmar and Vietnam reflect pragmatic strategies to ensure that the relationship benefits border regions in Yunnan as well as protecting China's broader strategic interests. China's approach to both Vietnam and Myanmar needs to be understood by the United States, particularly as U.S. foreign policy towards the two Southeast Asian nations shift.

In 2009, Secretary of State Hillary Clinton announced that the State Department was conducting a review of the country's policy towards Burma (as the U.S. government still refers to Myanmar). Recognizing that neither the U.S.' sanction-based strategy, or ASEAN's engagement-based strategy had improved the political situation in Myanmar, the U.S. determined that it would begin to engage the junta in Naypyitaw, while maintaining its strict sanctions policy. The U.S. felt that their dialogue with the Burmese

---

247.Interview, Yunnan 2010. The official was good-heartedly satirizing the Chinese Communist hero, Lei Feng who once wrote that he was like a screw that never gets rusty in a machine, implying that he was a tireless worker for the greater good.

government in 2009 and 2010 yielded virtually no results, culminating in the disappointing outcome of the elections in November 2010 in which the National League for Democracy was unable to participate, and government-backed parties secured more than 80% of available seats and the military retained a guaranteed 25% of both houses of parliament. Aung San Suu Kyi's release from house arrest following the election did little to satisfy critics, and the Assistant Secretary of State Kurt Campbell confirmed publicly in February that the U.S. would continue its sanctions policy. [248]

U.S. policy of isolating Myanmar is incompatible with China's strategy, which along with Russia publicly approved of the election. China's trade and investments in Myanmar effectively negate the impact of sanctions, though Myanmar undoubtedly suffers from them to some degree.. The U.S. inclination to try to engage the Burmese government aligns the U.S. to ASEAN and Chinese strategies, but the objective of China's geopolitical approach and the U.S.' ideological perspective are fundamentally different. China's economic engagement with Myanmar does not seek to influence the political system or improve the human rights situation in the country. China's investment in high-profile projects such as the oil and gas pipelines are first and foremost about addressing Chinese insecurities and concerns about local development. U.S. entreaties to Myanmar to reform its political system in exchange for economic benefits have been unsuccessful, not necessarily because of ASEAN's and China's conflicting strategy, but because of the political realities in Myanmar itself. Should conditions improve

---

248."U.S. Foreign Policy Goals and Objectives in Southeast Asia for 2011,"
Briefing by Assistant Secretary Kurt Campbell, State Department, February 2, 2011. Accessed at: http://www.state.gov/video/?videoid=774956482001

in Myanmar in the future, however, U.S. policy will have to shift quickly in response. Tangible, incremental inducements will be necessary for an engagement policy to be successful, giving the U.S. new influence and leverage in Myanmar. Chinese responses to possibly improving U.S.-Myanmar ties in the future will likely be marked by suspicion and possibly even counter-responses by China if they feel their privileged access and influence is threatened. Addressing these Chinese concerns will likely be necessary for a successful U.S.-Myanmar policy.

China's rise has particular relevance to Vietnam and their foreign policy calculations. Facing a more assertive China marked by a relentlessly modernizing PLA and heightened tensions over disputed maritime claims, Vietnam has responded by increasing its purchases of high tech weapons, primarily from Russia, and actively seeking to strengthen its relationship with the United States. In the 15 years since normalization of U.S.-Vietnam relations, past animosities have been addressed, trade and investment

---

249.U.S. Census Bureau, Selected Population Profile in the United States Population Group: Vietnamese alone or in any combination Data Set: 2007 American Community Survey 1-Year Estimates, available at: http://factfinder.census.gov/servlet/IPTable?_bm=y&-geo_id=01000US&-geo_id=NBSP&-qr_name=ACS_2007_1YR_G00_S0201&-qr_name=ACS_2007_1YR_G00_S0201PR&-qr_name=ACS_2007_1YR_G00_S0201T&-qr_name=ACS_2007_1YR_G00_S0201TPR&-ds_name=ACS_2007_1YR_G00_&-reg=ACS_2007_1YR_G00_S0201:048;ACS_2007_1YR_G00_S0201PR:048;ACS_2007_1YR_G00_S0201T:048;ACS_2007_1YR_G00_S0201TPR:048&-_lang=en&-redoLog=false&-format=

has flourished and people-to-people ties have deepened. Vietnam is actively pursuing a better relationship with the United States which will increasingly be marked by growing trade and substantive security cooperation. While Vietnam's motivation might superficially be driven by concern about a rising China, the U.S. is responding to Vietnamese overtures out of a national sense that strengthened relations are desirable in their own right. U.S. alliances elsewhere in Northeast and Southeast Asia were not formed because of China, and they remain relevant today because of a broad range of mutual interests that are far broader than a single country.

However, improving U.S.-Vietnam relations worry some in Beijing that the U.S. is seeking to contain China or forming alliances against it. The U.S. should craft a strategy to respond to Chinese concerns, incorporating a narrative that explains U.S. interests in Vietnam, not only in geostrategic terms, but local and pragmatic ones as well. The U.S. Census estimated in 2007 that there were 1.6 million Vietnamese-Americans, and Vietnamese-American groups highlight that they were the fastest growing ethnic group in the United States between 1990 and 2000.[249] Flights between the U.S. and Asian transportation hubs are often filled with Vietnamese-Americans visiting their ancestral homeland, strengthening family and professional ties between the two countries. The U.S.-Vietnam bilateral trade agreement came into effect in December 10, 2001, a day before China joined the WTO. Reminding China of America's cultural and economic links to Vietnam and emphasizing the benefits of U.S. engagement to Vietnam's economic development underscores the potential win-win-win for improving bilateral ties.

-V-

Conclusion: China's Multilayered Periphery Policy

From Beijing to the Border

As China has sought to both extend development from its coasts to the edge of its territorial limits, the post-Cold War geopolitical environment has largely proved conducive to an approach to development in which international trade and investment plays a leading role. At the same time, since the Cold War ended, China has been able to develop relationships with its territorial neighbors that are overall the best they have ever been. During the Cold War, China and many of its neighbors were at odds either over boundaries and or ideology; with the end of the Cold War China resolved nearly all of these barriers to cooperation with its neighbors. The post-Cold War international environment, including its new economic and security challenges, has also opened the door to new forms of engagement by the United States and other countries along China's territorial perimeter, potentially adding a new trigger for Beijing's latent border neuralgia.

With a vision of international trade and investment as key both to local development and to an economic interdependence conducive to regional stability, Chinese leaders have demonstrated a staunch commitment to keeping China's borders open. However, with openness comes external influence, with its increased potential to disrupt the domestic stability that is given existential importance by the Chinese regime. Non-traditional security threats are one facet of Chinese concerns, along trans-border ethnic nationalism that could undermine Beijing's control over border regions. Furthermore, U.S. (and to a much lesser degree Indian) engagement with nations on China's periphery can potentially heighten Chinese fears of hostile encirclement or foreign interference in its border region. As a result, China links foreign policy objectives and domestic development goals in its policy toward its territorial neighbors, and with its provinces, autonomous regions, or other localities along its borders. Each entity plays a critical role not only in China's policy calculations but as distinct policy actors as well.

How does this work in practice? Drawing on and building upon the preceding discussions focused on China's relations with North Korea, Mongolia, Myanmar and Vietnam, a number of structures and instruments, as well as policy drivers and flows appear most significant in China's relations with neighboring states.

Structures

Chinese foreign affairs are guided foremost by the Foreign Affairs Leading Small Group (FALSG) of the Communist Party (, Zhongyang Waishi Gongzuo Lingdao Xiaozu), also responsible for national security. The FALSG's membership is formally a secret but it presumed to include many of China's most senior leadership from policy areas involving China's foreign affairs and international security, including China's most senior leader, General Secretary Hu Jintao, who heads the group, State Councilor Dai Bingguo, its Secretary General, as well as Vice-President Xi Jinping. Included among the group's other members are such leaders as the Minister of National Defense and vice chairman of the Central Military Commission, the Minister of Public Security, key State Councilors, China's Foreign Minister, the Head of the International Liaison Department of the Central Committee, the Minister of Commerce, the Deputy Head of the PLA General Staff Department and Head of the PLA's Foreign Affairs Office. According to some sources, Premier Wen Jiabao is not a member of this group, although as was clear in the discussion of China's "good neighbor" policy, he clearly plays a role in articulating foreign policy principles and objectives.[250] Alongside and subordinate to this Party structure, the Ministry of Foreign Affairs oversees interactions with foreign governments and communicates Chinese interests to the world.

This central Party-state structure overseeing foreign policy and interactions with international actors is mirrored in the provincial and local levels, down to the county or district level. In Yunnan, for example, as is typical of other provinces and autonomous regions, foreign affairs are managed by the Yunnan Provincial Committee of the Communist Party of China (CPC) and its Foreign Affairs Leading Group. Formal bureaucratic structures within the Yunnan provincial government include its Foreign Affairs Office (FAO) and Foreign Trade and Economic Cooperation Commission (FTEC), with the former leading the political dimension of the province's external relationships and the

---

250.See Jeremy Paltiel, "Structure and Process in Chinese Foreign Policy, "Canadian International Council, Paper No. 8, (March 2010), available at http://www.onlinecic.org/resourcece/archives/chinapapers/chinapapersno8paltielpdf.

latter in charge of international economic ties. Individual bureaus under the governor's office at provincial also have direct contact with their counterparts across their borders, such as the civil affairs, public security, commerce, and presumably even intelligence or security organs such as the bureau of state security. Within the provincial government there are also other offices that play a role in managing the province's foreign relations, such as the Overseas Chinese Affairs Office, Taiwan Affairs Office, and CPC organs, such as the United Front Work Department and Propaganda Department. Quasi-governmental bodies, like the People's Friendship Association, also play a role in facilitating visits by nongovernmental actors to the province and its administrative regions. These organs are supported by the provincial government, but serve as the de facto agents of the central government. This political structure is generally mirrored at the prefecture or municipality-level as well as county levels below that. [251]

Provincial capitals and key cities also host foreign consulates. Vietnam, Thailand, Myanmar, Malaysia, Laos, and Cambodia, all have consulates in Yunnan's capital, not only supporting commercial flows through visas and investment information, but also playing a role in political exchanges.[252] Mongolia has a consulate-general in

251.Chen Zhimin, "Coastal Provinces and China's Foreign policy-making," in
Yufan Hao and Lin Su (eds.), China's Foreign Policy Making: Societal Force and Chinese American Policy (Aldershot,UK: Ashgate Publishing Limited: 2005), available on-line at http://www.irchina.org/en/pdf/czm5.pdf.

252. See, for example, the Vietnamese consulate in Kunming's report on the visit of provincial party secretary to Vietnam, "Yunnan Party Leader Welcomed to Vietnam," November 25, 2010, available at http://www.vietnamconsulate-kunming.org/en/nr070521165956/.

Inner Mongolia's Hohhot and Erlian has had an Office of Mongolia's Hohhot Consulate-General since cross-border trade between China and Mongolia began to accelerate in 1996.[253]

Chinese provinces also set up their own overseas offices in international capitals or key cities, often in the form of provincially-owned trading companies or trade associations. For example, Yunnan has a Representative Office of Yunnan Commerce in Rangoon, as well as a Yunnan Commerce Agency under the auspices of the Business Association of China in Hanoi; Inner Mongolia operates an Office of Trade and Investment in Ulan Bator, and as previously mentioned, Jinping County has a representative office in Vietnam's Dianbian city.

Local administrative organs also have responsibility for other aspects of the province's (or autonomous region's) affairs related to international issues. For example, provincial-level Ethnic and Religious Affairs commissions are tasked with " guid[ing] the religious circles to develop international exchange on the basis of friendship; resist[ing] the infiltration of hostile forces abroad, to publicize the national religious policies, and work in coordination with the concerned departments on foreign affairs with regard to religions..." and also "assist[ing] municipal or county governments in dealing with emergencies and problems affecting social stability."[254] Ethnic and Religious Affairs

253."China-Mongolia Relations, Foreign Ministry of the People'sRepublicofChina,May25,2010,availableathttp://www.chinadaily.com.cn/china/2010wentour/2010-05/27/content_9899648.htm

254.This language drawn from Zhejiang province's website, http://www.zhejiang.gov.cn/zjforeign/english/node500/node503/node507/index.html.

Commissions are also responsible for managing ethnic minority populations and in key jurisdictions in border areas are particularly powerful departments because of the large economic development budgets they control, such as the PBWM resources.

Border provinces also have government divisions specifically related to their work with contiguous states. For example, the Yunnan Foreign Affairs Office has a "Neighboring Countries Affairs Division" whose responsibilities are

> ... to implement guiding policies and principles of China to neighboring countries, instructions of provincial committee of CPC and provincial people's government on border affairs, treaties and protocols that Chinese government signed with neighboring countries on border line and border management and other international law; to manage, inspect and supervise the border line of Sino-Myanmar, Sino Vietnam and Sino-Laos; to deal with boundary affairs and promote friendship with neighboring countries; to provide guidance and join meetings in regard to boundary affairs; to assist related departments deal with affairs concerning about boundary affairs; to join negotiations on issues of border demarcation; to pass material and attitudes to related organizations such as ministry of foreign affairs on border negotiation issues; to investigate neighboring countries and border condition focus on economic development and opening up to outside world; to give suggestions and advice to superior departments on neighboring countries affairs.[255]

---

255. See Yunnan Foreign Affairs Office website, http://www.yfao.gov.cn/Enshow2.aspx?id=17.

Provincial level public security bureaus have responsibility for the local People's Armed Police frontier units and facilitate cooperation between them, local public security officers, the militia and PLA border defense forces. Work includes ensuring border security, preparing for emergency response scenarios and engaging in rural construction for poverty alleviation.[256] In Jilin this work is conducted under the guidance of the State Ethnic Affairs Commission and the PBWM program in coordination with the Provincial Economic and Trade Commission.[257]

These structures are also replicated within administrative divisions below the province, down to the county level. For example a prospective foreign investor in Yunnan interested in contact with authorities at the prefecture level could contact the Investment Promotion Bureau of Honghe Prefectural Government or the Dehong Prefecture Investment Promotion Office of Dehong Prefectural Government Economic Cooperation. At the county level, there is a Hekou County Administrative Committee for the Hekou Border Economic Cooperation Zone. In Ruili City, there is an Economic and Trade Bureau.[258] In Yanbian there is both a Rajin-Sonbong Zone Yanji Representative Office and a Hunchun City Economy Cooperation Bureau. Each of these local-level border jurisdictions have a "port office" (kouan bangongshi) within the local commerce bureau which coordinates policy and implementation at border crossings. There are also civil affairs bureaus; similarly, there are ethnic affairs commissions and public security offices at the local level that can interface with their counterparts across the border on various aspects of border control as needed.[259]

256." " , xbfm.jl.gov.cn/chengjiyujingyan/bianfang-2.htm -

257. ".. - ,"

258 Authors' visits to these border zones, 2010.

259 Authors were told in the course of their interviews that generally such meetings would be coordinated through the local foreign affairs office.

Instruments Coordinating Mechanisms

Informal mechanisms to bring bureaucratic agencies together to address policy issues that span the boundaries of a given government organ are a well-established dimension of the Chinese policy architecture. Leading small groups (lingdao xiaozu) provide ways to address policy areas (such as national security) or policy goals (such as the Western Development Leading Small group). Special committees may also be established as provisional mechanisms, particularly to gather experts and leaders in particular areas to consult on issues, such as those within the National People's Congress (NPC). Such mechanisms are utilized at both the national and subnational levels of China's governing structure.

Administrative Cooperation

Structured collaboration and partnerships across administrative areas are also used to produce policy results. For example, provinces or other subnational administrative entities may be assigned special relationships to central organs involved in foreign policy. The Chinese Foreign Ministry reportedly has seconded more than 60 of its diplomats to serve within local governments, including as vice-mayors, where they contribute expertise to help internationalize strategic thinking about economic development opportunities.[260] In the case of Yunnan, the Ministry of Foreign Affairs' Poverty Alleviation Office has responsibility for working directly with Jinping County, where one of its diplomats serves for generally two-year terms, with a key focus helping link international development programs to the county.[261] A member of

260.Freeman, discussion with members of the Vice-Mayor's office in Nanjing, 2010.

261.Shanghai also has special responsibility for supporting development in Yunnan and groups in Shanghai have cooperated with the MOFA in development activities in Jinping.

the foreign ministry routinely also serves in the Xinjiang foreign affairs office. At the subprovincial level, border security cooperation planning across agencies is carried out through routine planning meetings between the PAP and the PLA.–in Yunnan's Honghe, for example, this is every two months. Regular meetings among the PSB, the military affairs office, the foreign affairs office, and the immigration bureau also reportedly take place to manage illegal border crossing issues-- in Ruili the guideline is for such meetings to take place monthly at minimum.[262]

Bilateral cooperation frameworks are also used to facilitate cooperation between China's subnational administrative regions and their counterparts in border countries on certain issues. For example, in 2009, China and Laos established a liaison office within Kunming to facilitate law enforcement cooperation around human trafficking activities across their mutual border. Similarly, there is a narcotics control committee in Kunming to enable improved cooperation against drug smuggling and drug production in the China-Myanmar border areas.[263] Informal but routine cooperation is common across the border between local areas. Authorities in Jinping described regular cooperation between their offices of trade, tourism and culture and their counterpart offices in Vietnam, as well as monthly meetings on specific issues related to border trade and investment. Officials from the two sides (prefecture-level on the China side, provincial-level on the Vietnam side) hold annual meetings. While no formal joint border patrols have been organized along the Vietnam-China border, there are plans to do so as border demarcation work is completed. In Ruili, border police meet with their Myanmar counterparts through meetings coordinated by the local foreign office

262.Authors' discussions, 2010.

263.http://www.ibiblio.org/obl/docs3/BURMA_beyond_2000_chap3-China.pdf

and the two sides have cooperated on operations to counter human and drug trafficking operations and on planning for emergencies.[264]

Several border provinces are involved in multilateral frameworks for cooperation. Jilin and Inner Mongolia are both participants, with Jilin taking the lead among Chinese provinces, in the UNDP-organized Greater Tumen Initiative (GTI), which brings China together with several of its Northeast Asian neighbors to promote subregional initiatives that encourage economic growth, improve living standards and contribute to peace and stability in Northeast Asia.[265] Yunnan province has represented China in the Greater Mekong Subregion (GMS) project since 1992 and the organizations, such as specialized research institutes, that have formed in Yunnan to support its part in it have made Kunming a center of ASEAN expertise in China. Guangxi also joined Yunnan as a participant in GMS representing China in 2004. With assistance from the Asian Development Bank, the GMS brings together China, Cambodia, Lao PDR, Myanmar, Thailand and Vietnam to enhance regional competitiveness through infrastructure development and energy cooperation, as well as common initiatives to address environmental, health, and other social concerns.[266] Inner Mongolia and Xinjiang

264. Authors' interviews, 2010. Authors were told that in 2007 Ruili participated in a two-week joint exercise with Myanmar on anti-terrorism and flood control according to the terms of a border cooperation agreement negotiated by Luo Gan, then secretary of the Political and Legislative Affairs Committee of the CPC Central Committee, and former prime minister of Myanmar, Khin Nyunt.

265. Greater Tumen Initiative website, http://www.tumenprogramme.org/.

266. Asian Development Bank, Greater Mekong Subregion brochure, http://www.adb.org/Documents/Brochures/Devt-Effectiveness-Country-Briefs/Greater-Mekong-Subregion.pdf.

are also represented in the eight-country Central Asian Regional Economic Cooperation (CAREC) program.[267]

Financing

Fiscal flows are the most immediately potent instrument of the state in its efforts to secure its border region, and border provinces are eager beneficiaries. Provincial governments have representative offices in Beijing, as do many municipal and even prefectural governments (including Yanbian), which engage in lobbying activities.[268]

Major sources of financing domestic development (and infrastructure) in China's border regions are the WDP and linked PBWM programs. Since 2003, China's Northeast has been the beneficiary of the Revitalize the Northeast Industrial program targeting Jilin, Liaoning and Heilongjiang, and also including five prefectures in Inner Mongolia involving billions of dollars in central funding.[269] From 2000 to 2008, China's WDP alone funded the development of over 100 projects, valued at RMB1740 billion.[270] By 2008 the accumulated fixed assets investment in areas under the WDP program reached RMB 7,790 billion. Preferential fiscal policies include an exemption or reduced contribution by

267.Central Asia Regional Economic Cooperation (CAREC) website, http://www.adb.org/carec/about.asp.

268." 8,", November 1, 2010,available at: http://politics.people.com.cn/GB/99014/13102489.html.

269. "Policy for Revitalizing Old Industrial Bases of North East China, "available at http://amur-heilong.net/aic/en/1/06_economic_development/0605policyrevitalize/.

270. Doris Ma and Tim Summers, "Is China's Growth Moving Inland? A Decade of 'Develop the West' Centre for East Asian Studies," The Chinese University of Hong Kong, Asia Programme Paper: ASP PP 2009/02, October 2009, available at http://www.chathamhouse.org.uk/files/15082_1009pp_chinasgrowth.pdf.

minority areas to infrastructure development projects. [271] In addition, as a report on development of ethnic minority regions during the 11th Five Year Plan comments,

> ...[b]ecause of differences in history, culture, customs and religion, some ethnic minorities have special needs. For instance, the Tibetan, Mongolian, Uyghur and Kazak herdsmen need saddles, riding boots and brick tea, and the Muslims have their own special needs for Halal foods. To show respect for minority cultures and satisfy these special needs, the state has worked out preferential policies for the production of and trade in these items. ..In 2007 the state established a fund to ensure the production and promotion of the special commodities needed by the ethnic minorities, as well as related personnel training.

In 2006, a spokesman for the Leading Group for Western Development reported that 89.5 percent of villages covered by the WDP had been linked to highways, and 99% had been electrified.[272] In a report to the 18th session of the Standing Committee of the 11th National People's Congress (NPC) at the end of 2010, the State Ethnic Affairs Commission indicated that spending on poverty relief in ethnic minority regions reached RMB34.24 billion, with additional spending to accelerate economic and social development in the eight heavily minority provinces and autonomous regions since 2006, registering an annual increase of 28.9 percent,

---

271.Information Office of the State Council, "China's Ethnic Policy and Common Prosperity and Development of All Ethnic Groups," Sep. 27, 2009, available at http://en.showchina.org/China/WhitePapers/2009/201001/t525975_6.htm.

272."W. China Development Strategy Bears Fruit,"china.org.cn, August 31, 2006, available at http://www.china.org.cn/english/features/poverty/179749.htm.

reflecting an allocation of RMB 3.04 billion.[273] The Foreign Ministry reports that it contributed more than RMB19.4 million toward poverty alleviation in Yunnan in 2010 alone, with an additional RMB 1.2 million coming from the provincial foreign affairs office. The same source indicated that in 2009, Yunnan received RMB 3.2 billion in funding for poverty alleviation from a variety of sources.[274]

Other programs include funding associated with the 11th Five Year Plan for the Economic Development of the Borderlands, begun in 2005. In 2009 the government expanded this iteration of its "Borderlands Construction Plan," drafted in 1979 to all frontier counties and the frontier farms under the Xinjiang Production and Construction Corps. Official reports state that the central government had invested RMB1.446 billion and completed more than 20,000 projects in the borderlands under this plan.[275] In addition, during the 11th Five-year Plan period (2006-2010), central China's five autonomous regions and three provinces with large numbers of ethnic-minority inhabitants and the Xinjiang Production and Construction Corps received RMB913 to construct 23,400 comprehensive village and township cultural centers. [276]

Policy Flows

The structures, formal and informal, hint at the ways in which domestic and international security is linked in China's policy toward its periphery. The presence of diplomats from the foreign ministry in Yunnan and Xinjiang certainly presents one direct connection. Policy responses to particular circumstances offer insights into the way that

---

273.China spends US$5 bln on poverty relief for ethnic minorities

274. Freeman, interview, 2011.

275.Information Office of the State Council, (2009).

276.Information Office of the State Council (2009).

North Korea suspended its participation in GTI in 2009.

domestic stability and border security are linked.

The interaction between Jilin and central ministries in the Tumen project offers one example of this linkage. The initial vision for subregional cooperation around development of the Tumen delta came from Jilin. Academics from Jilin, who proposed the initiative, worked with the provincial government to sell their idea to Beijing, ultimately winning the political and financial support that enabled Jilin to play a key role in the UNDP-led international agreement to launch the Tumen program. China's representatives on the regional Consultative Commission for the Tumen project have included vice ministers from relevant Chinese ministries, including the National Development and Reform Commission (formerly the State Development Planning Commission) and Ministry of Commerce (formerly the Ministry of Foreign Trade and Economic Cooperation), with the vice governor of Jilin. These representatives interact with ministerial-level counterparts from other members states. Only the DPRK's "national team" also included a local representative from the Rajin-Sonbong People's Committee. A central-level Leading Group for Cooperation in Tumen River Area Development has included ministerial and provincial representation.[277]

China's approach to managing the clashes within Myanmar near its border and the ensuing refugee crisis offers a different example. In August 2009, Myanmar government forces attacked the Kokang army, an ethnic Chinese militia in Myanmar's Northwest Shan State. After fighting intensified, 37,000 refugees and remnants of the Kokang army fled to the Nansan border crossing in Lincang

---

277.Carla P. Freeman, "Neighborly Relations: the Tumen Development Project and China's Security Strategy," Journal of Contemporary China, Vol. 18.62 (January 2010):142; 145; 150.

Prefecture where Yunnan authorities rapidly mobilized the military and civilian resources to prevent chaos from spilling over the border onto Chinese territory.[278] Implementing an emergency management response mechanism that had been under development since the 2003 Severe Acute Respiratory Syndrome (SARS) outbreak, the Yunnan authorities followed a strategy established by the central government and adapted by the local government. By establishing clear responsibilities between the central, provincial, prefecture and country governments and each bureau within the various levels, the Yunnan-based military and civilian authorities effectively conducted security and relief operations, drawing on pre-positioned disaster relief supplies stocked by the central and local governments. To ensure that lines of communication between Yunnan and the central government were maintained, as they had not been in 2003 when the Beijing Municipal Government deceived the central government during the SARS outbreak, Minister of Public Security Meng Jianzhu was dispatched to the border area to oversee operations during the Kokang crisis.

However, the Kokang crisis which spilled onto Chinese territory also revealed the limits of China's foreign policy and security approach to its border. China's reluctance to interfere in Myanmar's internal affairs did little to prevent the crisis from occurring, and it is likely that such restraint in future crises in other border regions will have the same result. Efforts to secure the border through cross-border trade and investments in Chinese border counties focusing on social and economic development, including infrastructure, while successful at raising incomes, has done little to address traditional and non-traditional security threats in fragile states contiguous to China. To hedge against hard and soft security threats along the North Korean and Myanmar

278. Drew Thompson, "Border Burdens: China's Response to the Myanmar Refugee Crisis," China Security, Vol. 5 No. 3, 2009.

borders, China has given the PLA added responsibilities for border security. There, and along other borders, the government has pre-positioned disaster relief supplies, improved security infrastructure and prepared extensively to respond to future contingencies. Nonetheless, the crisis underscored the key role played by provincial and local governments in managing cross-border relationships, offering an example of the degree to which security (including human security_ along China's borders rests on the capacity of China's subnational governments.[279]

Along other Chinese Borders: Patterns amid Challenges

This study has focused on China's smaller neighbors that, unlike Russia or India, are not China's strategic competitors in the region. Nonetheless, they all pose security challenges for China that are manifested on the ground in China's border provinces, many that have the potential to influence China's domestic stability. Other Chinese neighbors on China's western front present similar if not greater challenges, yet Beijing has supported local efforts to reach across the border to engage in trade with its neighbors. Despite concerns about terrorist networks, China and Pakistan have pursued deeper cooperation across their mutual border at China's Xinjiang Autonomous Region. The two sides have worked together to facilitate trade through improved banking cooperation and currency settlement arrangements and Xinjiang has been upgrading roads and border ports. During a visit to Xinjiang by Pakistan's Ambassador to China to sign a friendly relations agreement with Xinjiang Autonomous Region, the Region's Chairman, Nur Bekri, made his views on Xinjiang's role China's bilateral relationship with Pakistan clear: "As the closest neighboring

279.Carla Freeman, "Fragile Edges between Security and Insecurity: China's Border Regions," in Rongxing Guo and Carla Freeman (eds.), Managing Fragile Regions: Method and Application, (New York, Springer, 2010): 41.

province of Pakistan, Xinjiang is obliged to contribute to the firming up of our diplomatic relationship."[280]

Xinjiang's ties with Pakistan are part of a broader framework for economic outreach by China through Xinjiang to Central Asia articulated in the early 2000s. Xinjiang began signing cooperation agreements with and developing its border ports along its 5,600 kilometer border with Mongolia, Russia, Kazakhstan, Kyrgyzstan, Tajikistan, Afghanistan, Pakistan and India with the goal of becoming a "bridgehead to Central Asia." By 2005, its Alataw Pass Port had already become China's second largest trading port on land and Xinjiang companies had invested nearly USD2 billion in Central Asia.[281]

Tibet, which hosts a consulate from Nepal, has played a role in boosting Beijing's economic relationship with Kathmandu. Amid other moves by Beijing to strengthen the bilateral relationship, including an increase in its military assistance to Nepal, the two sides have also taken measures to facilitate border cooperation. Enhancing conditions for cross-border trade through simplified customs procedures and other logistics has been one side of this move. There is also clearly an ethnic dimension to improved border cooperation between Tibet and Nepal, which is home to a substantial community of Tibetan refugees. In March 2010, China organized an "interaction" on Nepal and Tibet on the second "Serfs Emancipation Day," and invited Nepali diplomats to observe a session of the Ninth Tibet Autonomous Region People's Political Consultative

---

280. Lie Xiaoxun, "Xinjiang, Pakistan Sign Friendly Relations Agreement," China Daily, April 8, 2009, available at http://www2.chinadaily.com.cn/china/2009-04/08/content_7768269.htm..

281. "Xinjiang Becomes Bridgehead for Trade Ties with Central Asia," Xinhua, September 23, 2005, available at http://www.china.org.cn/english/BAT/143261.htm.

Conference.[282] Human rights observers are concerned about the implications of these closer ties for the Tibetan refugees in Nepal. In June 2010, Nepal is alleged to have returned three Tibetan refugees from China, the first case of such refoulement since 2003, at a time when Nepal had tightened security along its side of the border.[283]

U.S. Interests

As the world's dominant power, the U.S. has interests both within China and in the countries that surround it, and China may not like that U.S. interests straddle the steles that mark China's political boundaries, but it must live with this for now. Crafting a comprehensive U.S. policy that incorporates better appreciation for China's security concerns in its border regions would refute Chinese sentiments in some quarters that the U.S. seeks to contain and weaken it. The last thing the U.S. wants to see is a failed state the size of China, and it is a mistake for Chinese analysts to conclude that U.S. support to minority groups within China reflects this objective.

---

282. "Interaction on "Relationship between Nepal and China's Tibet" held in Nepal," China Daily, March 26, 2010, available at http://english.peopledaily.com.cn/90001/90776/90883/6932284.html; "Nepal Wishes to Strengthen Relations with China," Xinhua, February 3, 2010, available at http://www.chinadaily.com.cn/china/2010-02/03/content_9423729.htm.
283. "Kathmandu and Beijing Tighten Grip on Refugees," Spero News, December 6, 2010, available at http://www.speroforum.com/site/article.asp?id=44525&t=Nepal%3A++China%3A+++Kathmandu+and+Beijing+tighten+grip+on+Tibetan+refugees; "Pushed by China, Tibetans Leave Nepal," Global Post, April 12, 2010 available at http://www.theinvestigativefund.org/investigations/international/1276/pushed_by_china,_tibetans_leave_nepal

The U.S. is not ignorant of latent mutual mistrust, particularly China's perception of U.S. strategy towards states on China's periphery. In Secretary of State Hillary Clinton's seminal speech in memory of Ambassador Richard Holbrook, she attempted to address the new approach that the U.S. has towards China and the "international landscape":

> In the 21st century, it does not make sense to apply zero-sum 19th century theories of how major powers interact. We are moving through uncharted territory. We need new ways of understanding the shifting dynamics of the international landscape, a landscape marked by emerging centers of influence, but also by non-traditional, even non-state actors, and the unprecedented challenges and opportunities created by globalization. This is a fact that we believe is especially applicable to the U.S-China relationship. Our engagement–indeed, I would say our entanglement–can only be understood in the context of this new and more complicated landscape.[284]

Despite Chinese misgivings about the U.S. presence in virtually every country bordering China, we share numerous mutual interests, partially suppressing transnational crime, preventing failed states from harboring non-traditional security threats, stemming the spread of radical Islam and extremism in Central Asia, and promoting investment in infrastructure which ensures the free flow of commerce that advances economic development and stability throughout East, South and Central Asia.

284.Remarks by Secretary of State Hillary Rodham Clinton, "Inaugural Richard C. Holbrooke Lecture on a Broad Vision of U.S.-China Relations in the 21st Century," January 14, 2011. Accessed at: http://www.state.gov/secretary/rm/2011/01/154653.htm

Therefore, the U.S. and China have a common set of objectives that they can jointly pursue, provided they share a common perspective on border regions, one that they currently do not. The U.S. needs to appreciate China's comprehensive, almost holistic security strategy if we are to make progress on critical issues of mutual interest on China's periphery.

Firstly, the actual border is a critical locus where the U.S. would gain by supporting China's efforts to strengthen border security. Boosting joint counter narcotics efforts, intelligence sharing, and other programs to stem transnational threats, including infectious disease should all be supported.

Secondly, U.S. involvement needs to be extended beyond the border line. For instance, China's strategy to promote border trade should be embraced and supported by the U.S. as part of a comprehensive strategy to build economic stability and resiliency, particularly in fragile parts of Asia. The U.S. government could increase support to countries on China's periphery so they can more rapidly develop infrastructure that keeps pace with the vast amounts of concrete poured on the Chinese side, so that greater commercial flows contribute to regional prosperity and the resulting security that it brings. Additionally, China and the U.S. share a mutual interest in improving governance in countries along its border, creating opportunities for joint programs that encourage economic and political liberalization that does not exclude either power and strengthens international regimes and norms that the U.S. and China both subscribe to and benefit from. This approach creates a framework which could contribute to the formulation of a new U.S. Burma policy that engages the country effectively for the benefit of its people, encourages behavior change on the part of its government, while assuring China that U.S. intentions do not run counter to its own interests.

This is by no means an easy task for the U.S. There are hazards to developing this strategy which can be identified and avoided. For instance, the U.S. needs to avoid becoming entangled in maritime and land border disputes, whether vast tracts of mountains claimed by China and India or the overlapping claims to swaths of the seas around China. The U.S. interests in promoting human rights and religious freedom in China will have to be incorporated, as part of U.S. overarching objectives for the region and bilateral relationship.

This broad agenda, encompassing China's border regions and both nations' complex relationships with neighboring countries can be furthered by a U.S.-China dialogue that incorporates both the economic and security issues that are reflected in China's complex outlook on its border regions. We ignore China's perspective of this critical nexus of its domestic and international security at our own peril. When a Chinese foreign ministry spokesperson states that China is "hurt" by U.S., or French or Australian engagements with either the Dalai Lama or Rebyia Kadeer, he fails to articulate China's deep insecurities about its own diversity and neighborhood. This does not mean that the U.S. should ignore exiles or disparate voices within China. However, U.S. policy formulation would greatly benefit from a deeper understanding of how minorities, the border region and neighboring countries shape China's own calculations about its power, its strategy and policies and ultimately, its image of itself.

China's relations with neighbor states are inexorably linked to Beijing's concerns about stability in its own border regions. It is important to remember that while China's is not a federal government, power in the Chinese political system is decentralized, making provinces and local-level government critical actors in many sectors. It is local governments who collect taxes and provide services, not the central government. Local governments are the engine that powers China's neighbor state relations, operating under aegis of the central government the invisible hand with its light touch. Customs officers at border crossings are employed by provincial governments and though they follow standards set by the central government, the duties they collect, like their loyalties are for local authorities. This devolution of power is of critical importance when seeking to divine "China's" intentions and strategies towards other countries. The central government can set the tone for bilateral relations, but the provinces and localities create limits on Beijing's maneuverability, assuring that the central and local government's policies are mutually reinforcing, pragmatic and focused on economic development and domestic stability. This political inter dependence and fiscal decentralization create an unwillingness of one level of the Chinese political system to disregard the interests of another, setting Chinese policy off on a predictably risk averse course. While this Chinese approach eschews ideology or principled intrusion in other countries' domestic affairs, it provides a predictable basis that the U.S. can use to shape and plan its own policies towards countries on China's periphery.

Bibliography

English Language

Amer, Ramses, *The Challenge of Managing Border Disputes between China and Vietnam,* (EAI Working Paper, Singapore: East Asian Institute, National University of Singapore, 1998.)

--- *The Ethnic Chinese in Vietnam and Relations,* (Kuala Lumpur, Forum, 1991.)

---"Assessing Sino-Vietnamese Relations through the Management of Contentious Issues," *Contemporary Southeast Asia,* 26: 2 (2004): 320-345.

Anderson, Malcom, *Frontiers: Territory and State Formation in the Modern World,* (Cambridge: Polity Press, 1996).

Atzili, Boaz, "When Good Fences Make Bad Neighbors," *International Security,* Vol. 31.3 (Winter 2006/07): 139-173.

Batchimeg, Migeddorj , "Future Challenges for the PRC and Mongolia: A Mongolia Perspective," *China Brief,* Volume 5, Issue 10 (May 05, 2005).

Barnett, A. Doak, *The Making of Foreign Policy in China: Structures and Process,* (Washington DC, Johns Hopkins Foreign Policy Institute, 1985).

Bedeski, Robert ´., "Mongolian Futures: Scenarios for a Landlocked State", *Asia Paper,* (Stockholm-Nacka, Sweden, and Washington DC: Institute for Security and Development Policy, 2008)

Blum, Susan D., Portraits of *'Primitives': Ordering Human Kinds in the Chinese Nation,* (Lanham, Rowman & Littlefield, 2001).

Blum, Susan D. and Lionel M. Jensen, *China Off Center: Mapping the Margins of the Middle Kingdom,* (University of Hawaii Press, 2002).

Breslin, Shaun, (ed.), *Microregionalism and World Order,* (Basingstoke, Palgrave, 2002).

Brown, Kerry, *The Purge of the Inner Mongolian People's Party in the Chinese Cultural Revolution, 1967–69: A Function of Language, Power and Violence,* (Kent, UK: GlobalOriental, 2006).

Bulag, Uradyn, *The Mongols at China's Edge: History & the Politics of National Unity* (Lanham: Rowman & Littlefield, 2002).

-- - "Mongolian Ethnicity and Linguistic Anxiety in China," *American Anthropologist,* Volume 5, Issue 4 (December 2003): 753–763.

--- , "Mongolia in 2008: From Mongolia to Mine-golia," *Asian Survey,* Vol. 49, Issue 1 (2009): 129-134.

Buzan, Barry. '"Change and Insecurity' Reconsidered." *Contemporary Security Policy,* 20. 3 ,(1999).

Cameron, David M., (ed.), *The Fragmented State: Regionalism and Supranationalism,* (Quebec, The Institute for Research on Public Policy and Policy Studies Institute, 1981).

Carlson, Allen, "Constructing the Dragon's Scales: China's Approach to Territorial Sovereignty and Border

Relations," *Journal of Contemporary China,* 12(37), (November , 2003): 677–698.

Chai, C. H. and Y. Y. Kueh, Clement Allan Tisdell (eds.), *China and the Asia Pacific Economy,* (New York, Nova Science Publishers, 1997).

Chang, Luke T., *China's Boundary Treaties and Frontier Disputes,* (London and New York, Oceana Publications, 1982).

Chen, Xiangming. *As Borders Bend: Transnational Spaces on the Pacific Rim,* (Lanham, MD., Rowman & Littlefield Publishers, Inc., 2005).

Cheng Xiaohe, "The Evolution of Sino-North Korean Relations in the 1960s," *Asian Perspective,* (Vol. 34, No.2, 2010): 173-199.

Cheung, Peter T.Y. and James T.H. Tang, "The External Relations of China's Provinces," in Lampton, David M. (ed.), *The Making of Chinese Foreign and Security Policy in the Era of Reform,* 1978-2000, (Stanford: Stanford University Press, 2001)

Christoffersen, Gaye, "Nesting the Sino-Russian Border and the Tumen Project in the Asia-Pacific: Heilongjiang's Regional Relations," *Asian Perspective* (Vol. 20, No. 2, Fall-winter 1996).

Chung Chien-peng, *Domestic Politics, International Bargaining & China's Territorial Disputes,* (London and New York, Routledge, 2004).

--- The "Good Neighbour Policy" in the Context of *China's Foreign Relations," China: An International Journal,* 7 (1), (March 2009): 107-123.

Chung, Jae Ho, "Studies of Central-Provincial Relations in the PRC: A Mid-Term Appraisal," *The China Quarterly,* No. 142, June 1995.

____*Central Control and Local Discretion in China: Leadership and Implementation during Post-Mao Decollectivization* (Oxford University Press, 2000)

----, "China's 'Soft Clash' with South Korea: The History War and Beyond," *Asian Survey,* (Vol. 49, Issue 3, 2009): 468–483.

Colin, Sebastien , 'A Border opening onto Numerous Geopolitical Issues," *China Perspectives,* 48 (2003),

Cotton, James , "China and Tumen River Cooperation: Jilin's Coastal Development Strategy," *Asian Survey,* Vol. 36, No. 11 (November 1996).

---- *Crossing Borders in the Asia Pacific: Essays on the Domestic-Foreign Policy Divide,* (New York: Nova Science Publishers, 2002).

Davis, David R. and Will H. Moore, "Ethnicity Matters: Transnational Ethnic Alliances and Foreign Policy Behavior," *International Studies Quarterly,* 41.1, 1997: 171-184.

Davies, Ian, "Regional Cooperation in Northeast Asia- The Tumen River Area Davelopment Program, 1990-2000," North Pacific Policy Papers #4 (Vancouver: Institute of Asian Research, 2000).

Di Cosmo, Nicola (ed.), *Military Culture in Imperial China,* (Cambridge: Harvard University Press, 2009).

Dresner, Daniel W. (ed.), *Locating the Proper Authorities: The Interaction of Domestic and International Institutions,* (Ann Arbor: University of Michigan, 2003).

Dreyer, June, "China's Minority Nationalities in the Cultural Revolution," *China Quarterly,* No. 55, (July-Sept., 1968): 96-109.

--- "China's Vulnerability to Minority Separatism," *Asian Affairs: An American Review* 32. 2 (Summer 2005).

Duara, Pransenjit, "De-Constructing the Chinese Nation," *The Australian Journal of Chinese Affairs,* No. 30, 1993.

----, "Provincial Narratives of the Nation," in Harumi Befu, *Cultural Nationalism in East Asia,* (Berkeley: Institute of East Asian Studies, 1992).

Duchachek, Ivo, Daniel Latouche, and Garth Stevenson (eds.), *Perforated Sovereignties and International Relations: Trans-Sovereign Contacts of Subnational Governments,* (Westport, CT., Greenwood, 1988).

Duiker, William J., *China & Vietnam: Roots of Conflict,* (Berkeley, CA: Institute of East Asian Studies, University of California, 1986).

Edwards, R. Randle, "Imperial China's Border Control Law," *Journal of Chinese Legal Studies* (Vol 1.1 Spring 1987).

Evans, Grant, Christopher Hutton and Kuah Khun Eng (eds.), *Where China Meets Southeast Asia: Social and Cultural Change in the Border Region,* (New York, Palgrave, 2000).

Eftimiades, Nicholas, *Chinese Intelligence Operations,* (United States, Reed Business Information, Inc., 1994).

Fang Gao, "What it Means to be a 'Model Minority': Voices of Ethnic Koreans in Northeast China," *Asian Ethnicity,* (Vol. 9, No. 1, February 2008).

Fitzgerald, John, (ed.), *Rethinking China's Provinces,* (London and New York, Routledge, 2002).

Fontana, Mary Anne, *Strategic Construction: An analysis of China's policy towards Four Frontier Regions* Ph.D. Dissertation (University of Pennsylvania, 1998).

Fuchs, Lawrence H., "Minority Groups and Foreign

Policy," *Political Science Quarterly*, Vol. 74.2 (June, 1959): 161-175.

Fravel, M. Taylor, *Strong Borders, Secure Nation: Cooperation and Conflict in China's Territorial Disputes*, (Princeton: Princeton University Press, 2008).

--- "Securing Borders: China's Doctrine and Force Structure for Frontier Defense," *The Journal of Strategic Studies*, Vol. 30.4-5, (August-October 2007): 705-737.

Freeman, Carla. *China's Reform Challenge: The Political-Economy of Reform in Northeast China, 1978-1998*, (Baltimore, Johns Hopkins University dissertation, 1998).

--- "Neighborly Relations: the Tumen Development Project and China's Security Strategy," *Journal of Contemporary China*, Vol. 19, No. 63, (2010).

Ganster, Paul and David E. Lorey, (eds.), *Borders and Border Politics in a Globalizing World*, (Lanham, MD: SR Books, 2005).

Gladney, Dru C., *Dislocating China: Muslims, Minorities, and Other Subaltern Subjects*, (Chicago, The University of Chicago Press, 2003).

--"Representing Nationality in China: Reforging Majority/ Minority Identities," *Journal of Asian Politics*, 53.1 (1994): 92-123.

Godwin, Paul H. B, "From Continent to Periphery: PLA Doctrine, Strategy and Capabilities Towards 2000," *The China Quarterly*, No. 146, (June,1996): 464-487.

Goldstein, Avery, *Rising to the Challenge: China's Grand Strategy and International Security*, (Stanford; Stanford University Press, 2005).

Goodman, David and Gerald Segal (eds.), *China Deconstructs: Politics, Trade and Regionalism*, (London and New York, Routledge, 1994).

Goodman, David (ed.), *China's Provinces in Reform: Class, Community, and Political Culture,* (New York, Routledge, 1997).

Goodman, David S.G. (ed.) *China's Campaign to 'Open Up to the West': National, Provincial-level and Local Perspective* (Cambridge: Cambridge University Press, 2004).

Grayson, Robin and Chimed-Erdene Baatar, "Remote Sensing of Cross-Border Routes between Mongolia and China," *World Placer Journal,* Vol. 9 (2009).

Guo, Rongxing and Carla Freeman (eds.), *Managing Fragile Regions: Method and Application,* (New York, Springer, 2010).

Gurr, Ted Robert, *People's Versus States: Minorities at Risk in the New Century,* (Washington DC, United States Institute of Peace, 2000).

Haggard, Stephen and Marcus Noland, *Famine in North Korea: Markets, Aid, and Reform,* (New York: Columbia University Press, 2007).

Hao, Yufan and Lin Su (eds.), *China's Foreign Policy Making: Societal Force and Chinese American Policy* (Aldershot,UK: Ashgate Publishing Limited: 2005).

Harrell, Stevan (ed.), *Cultural Encounters on China's Ethnic Frontiers,* (Seattle, University of Washington, 1995).

Heberer, Thomas, *China and Its National Minorities: Autonomy or Assimilation?* (Armonk, New York, East Gate, 1989).

Heberer, Thomas and Timothy Gluckman, *Private Entrepreneurs in China and Vietnam: Social and Political Functioning of Strategic Groups,* (Leiden, Brill, 2003).

Hesengerth, Oliver, *Regionalism in China-Vietnam Relations Institution-Building in the Greater Mekong Subregion,*

(UK: Routledge, 2009).

Hirschman, A., *National Power and the Structure of Foreign Trade* (Berkeley, C.A.: Berkeley University Press, ([1945] 1980).

Hu Angang and Meng Honghua, "The Rising of Modern China: Comprehensive National Power and Grand Strategy," (paper presented at KIEP Conference on "Rising China and the East Asian Economy" in Seoul on March 19-20, 2004).

Jakobson, Linda and Dean Knox, "New Foreign Policy Actors in China,"
SIPRI Policy Paper No. 26, September 2010.

Janowiak, William R., "The Last Hurrah? Political Protest in Inner Mongolia," *The Australian Journal of Chinese Affairs*, No. 19/20 (Jan-July, 1988): 269-288.

Jia Hao and Zhimin Lin, (eds.), *Changing Central-Local Relations in China: Reform and State Capacity*, (Boulder, Westview, 1994).

Johnston, Alastair Ian, *Cultural Realism: Strategic Culture and Grand Strategy in Chinese History*, (Princeton: Princeton University Press, 1995).

Kim, Jae Cheol , "The Political Economy of Chinese Investment in North Korea: A Preliminary Assessment," *Asian Survey*, Vol. 46, Issue 6 (2006).

King, Charles and Neil Melvin, "Diaspora Politics: Ethnic Linkages, Foreign Policy, and Security in Eurasia," *International Security*, Vol. 24, No. 3 (Winter 1999/2000): pp. 108–138.

Kiyoshi, Hasegawa, "Ethnic Tourism and Cultural Change in the Border Region of Yunnan Province: A Case Study on Xishuangbanna Dai Autonomous Prefecture," Center for Southeast Asian Studies of Kyoto University, 2000.

Lachapelle, Guy and Stéphane Paquin, *Mastering Globalization: New Sub-states' Governance And Strategies,* (New York, Routledge, 2005).

Laruelle, Marlene and Sebastien Peyrouse, "China as a Neighbor: Central Asian Perspectives and Strategies," (Central Asia-Caucasus Institute & Silk Road Studies Program, A Joint Transatlantic Research and Policy Center, Johns Hopkins University, 2009).

Lary, Diana (ed.), *The Chinese State at the Borders,* (Vancouver, The University of British Columbia Press, 2007).

Lattimore, Owen, "Origins of the Great Wall of China: A Frontier Concept in Theory and Practice," *Geographical Review,* Vol. 27. 4, (1937).

---- "The New Political Geography of Inner Asia," The *Geographical Journal,* Vol. 119.1, (1953).

Li Dunqiu, "Economic and Social Implications of China DPRK Border Trade for China's Northeast," National Bureau of Asian Research (2006).

Lieberthal, Kenneth G. and David M. Lampton, (eds.), Bureaucracy, Politics, and Decision Making in Post-Mao China, (Berkeley: University of California Press, 1992).

Linz, Juan J. and Amando de Miguel, "Within-Nation Differences and Comparisons: The Eight Spains" in R. L. Merritt and S. Rokkan (eds.), Comparing Nations: The Use of Quantitative Data in Cross-National Re-search, (New Haven: Yale University Press, 1966).

Ling, L.H.M., "Borders of Our Minds: Territories, Boundaries, and Power in the Confucian Tradition," in Buchanan, Allen and Margaret Moore, (eds.), *States, Nations, and Borders: The Ethics of Making Boundaries,* (Cambridge University Press 2003).

Lu, Ning, *The Dynamics of Foreign-policy Decision Making in China*, (New York, Perseus Publishing, 2000).

Luova, Outi , *Ethnic Transnational Capital Transfers and Development-Utilization of Ties with South Korea in the Yanbian Korean Autonomous Region*, (Turku, Finland, Turun Yliopisto, 2007).

----"Transnational Linkages and Development Initiatives in Ethnic Korean Yanbian, Northeast China: "Sweet and Sour" Capital Transfers," *Pacific Affairs*, (Vol. 82, No. 3 Fall 2009).

Lutterbeck, Derek, "Policing Migration in the Mediterranean," *Mediterranean Politics*, Vol.11.1, (March 2006): 59-82.

Ma, Doris and Tim Summers, "Is China's Growth Moving Inland? A Decade of 'Develop the West' Centre for East Asian Studies," The Chinese University of Hong Kong, Asia Programme Paper: ASP PP 2009/02, (October 2009).

Ma Yin, *China's Minority Nationalities*, (Beijing, Foreign Languages Press, 1989).

Mackerras, Colin, *China's Minorities: Integration and Modernization in the Twentieth Century*, (Hong Kong, Oxford University Press, 1994).

Matthew, Richard A. and Leah Fraser, "Global Environmental Change and Human Security: Conceptual and Theoretical Issues," *Global Environmental Change and Human Security Program Office*, University of California Irvine, November 2002.

McClain, Paula D., (ed.), *Minority Group Influence: Agenda Setting, Formulation and Public Policy*, (Westport, Greenwood Press, 1993).

Migdal, Joel (ed.), *Boundaries and Belonging: States and Societies in the Struggle to Shape Identities and Local*

Practices, (Cambridge, UK and New York: Cambridge University Press, 2004).

Ming Liu, "China and the North Korean Crisis: Facing Test and Transition," *Pacific Affairs,* Vol. 76, No. 3 (Fall, 2003).

Moodie, A.E., *Geography behind Politics,* (Hutchison's University Library, 1947).

Moore, Will H., "Ethnic Minorities and Foreign Policy," *SAIS Review* 22.2 (2002): 77-91.

Mosely, George, "China's Fresh Approach to the National Minority Question," *The China Quarterly,* No. 24 (Oct-Dec.,1965): 15-27.

Mullaney, Thomas, "Ethnic Classification Writ Large: The 1954 Yunnan Province Ethnic Classification Project and Its Foundations in Republican-Era Taxonomic Thought," *China Information,* 18.2004: 207-241.

Naughton, Barry J. and Dali L. Yang (eds.), *Holding China Together: Diversity and National Integration in the Post-Deng Era,* (Cambridge, UK: Cambridge University Press, 2004).

Newman, David, (ed.), *Boundaries, Territory, and Postmodernity,* (London: Frank Cass Publishers, 1999).

Nyamtseren, Lhamsurengiin, *Political, Security, Economic and Infrastructure Factors of Economic Cooperation in the Northeast Asia,* (Ulaanbaator, Mongolia, Mongolian Development Research Center, 2002).

Nyiri, Pal and Joana Breidenbach, *China Inside Out,* (Budapest: Central European Press, 2005),

O'Donnell, Guillermo, *Counterpoints: Selected Essays on Authoritarianism and Democratization,* (Notre Dame, IN: University of Notre Dame Press, 1999).

O'Dowd, Liam. "The Changing Significance of European Borders," In *New Borders for a Changing Europe,* edited by James Anderson, Liam O'Dowd and Thomas M. Wilson, (London: Frank Cass, 2003).

Park, John S. , "North Korea, Inc.: Gaining Insights into North Korean Regime Stability from Recent Commercial Activities," *US Institute of Peace Working Paper,* (April 22, 2009).

Peng Guangqian, Yao Youzhi (eds.), *The Science of Military Strategy,* (Beijing, Military Science Publishing House, 2005).

Percival, Bronson, *The Dragon Looks South: China and Southeast Asia in the New Century,* (Westport and London, Praeger Security International, 2007).

Pinilla, Daniel Gomez, " Border Disputes between China and North Korea," *China Perspectives,* Vol. 52 (2004).

Perkmann, Markus and Ngai-Ling Sum, *Globalization, Regionalization and Cross-Border Regions: Discourses and Governance,* (New York: Palgrave MacMillan, 2002).

Putnam, Robert D., "Diplomacy and Domestic Politics: The Logic of Two-Level Games," *International Organization* Summer, 1988.42: 427-460.

Rosenau, James. *Along the Domestic-Foreign Frontier: Exploring Governance in a Turbulent World,* (New York and Cambridge: Cambridge University Press, 1997).

Rossabi, Morris (ed.), *Governing China's Multiethnic Frontiers,* (Seattle, University of Washington Press, 2004).

---, *Modern Mongolia: from Khans to Commissars to Capitalists* (University of California Press, 2005).

Rozman, Gilbert, *Northeast Asia's Stunted Regionalism: Bilateral Distrust in the Shadow of Globalization,* (Cambridge, New York, and Melbourne: Cambridge University Press, 2004).

Scalapino, Robert A. "China's Relations with Its Neighbors," *Proceedings of the Academy of Political Science*, Vol. 38, No. 2, The China Challenge: American Policies in East Asia (1991).

Scobell, Andrew, *China and North Korea: From Comrades-In Arms to Allies at Arm's Length,* (Carlisle, PA, Strategic Studies Institute, 2004).

Shambaugh, David (ed.), *Power Shift: China and Asia's New Dynamics,* (Berkeley and Los Angeles: University of California Press, 2005).

Shirk, Susan, *The Political Logic of Economic Reform in China* (Berkeley: University of California Press, 1993.)

--- *China: Fragile Superpower,* (New York: Oxford, 2007).

Sneath, David, "The Impact of the Cultural Revolution in China on the Mongolians of Inner Mongolia," *Modern Asian Studies,* Vol. 28, No. 2 (May, 1994).

---, *Changing Inner Mongolia: Pastoral Nomad Society and the Chinese State,* (Oxford: Oxford University Press, 2000.)

Snyder, Richard, "Scaling Down: The Subnational Comparative Method," *Studies in Comparative International Development,* Spring 2001: 93-110.

Solinger, Dorothy, *Regional Government and Political Integration in Southwest China, 1949-1979,* (Berkeley: University of California Press, 1977).

Starr, S. Frederick (ed.), *The New Silk Road: Transport and Trade in Greater Central Asia,* (Washington DC , Central Asia-Caucasus Institute, Silk Road Studies Program, 2007).

Swaine, Michael D., *China: Domestic Change and Foreign Policy,* (National Defense Research Institute, 1995).

Swaine, Michael D. and Ashley J. Tellis, *Interpreting China's Grand Strategy: Past, Present and Future,* (Rand, 2000).

Tanner, Murray Scot and Eric Green, "Principals and Secret Agents: Central versus Local Control Over Policing and Obstacles to 'Rule of Law' in China," *The China Quarterly,* No. 191, (September 2007): 644-670.

Thompson, Drew and Carla Freeman, "Flood Across the Border: China's Disaster Relief Operations and Potential Response to a North Korean Refugee Crisis", US-Korea Institute and The Nixon Center (2009).

---, "Border Burdens: China's Response to the Myanmar Refugee Crisis," *China Security,* Vol. 5 No. 3, (2009).

Wachman, Alan M. "Suffering what it Must? Mongolia and the Power of the Weak," *Orbis:* Vol. 54, No. 4 (2010).

Waldron, Arthur, *The Great Wall of China: From History to Myth,* (New York: Cambridge University Press, 1990).

Wang Peiran, "*Sino-Mongolian Military Relations,*" China Security, Vol. 5.2 (2009).

Watson, Andrew, *Mao Zedong and the Political Economy of the Border Region,* (Cambridge: Cambridge University Press, 1980).

Watson, Francis, *The Frontiers of China,* (New York: Frederick Praeger, 1966).

Williams, Dee Mack, *Beyond Great Walls: Environment, Identity, and Development on the Chinese Grasslands of Inner Mongolia,* (Stanford: Stanford University Press, 2002.)

Wilson, Thomas M. and Hastings Donnan, *Border Identities: Nation and State in International Frontiers,* (Cambridge: Cambridge University Press, 1998).

Yan Xiao, Sibylle Kristensen, Jiangping Sun, Lin Lu, and Sten H. Vermund, "Expansion of HIV/AIDS in China: Lessons from Yunnan Province," *Soc Sci Med.* Volume 64(3) (February 2007): 665–675.

Yang, Richard, *Chinese Regionalism: The Security Dimension,* (Boulder: Westview, 1994).

Zhan, Xiaohong "Analysis of South Korea's Direct Investment in China," *China & World Economy* : 94-104, Vol. 13, No. 1, 2005.

Zhang Yongjin and Roubin Azizian, Ethnic Challenges beyond Borders: Chinese and Russian Perspectives on the Central Asian Conundrum, (Palgrave Macmillan, Ltd., 1998).

Zhao, Suisheng (ed.), *China-U.S. Relations Transformed: Perspectives and Strategic Interactions* (Routledge, UK: 2008).

Zheng Yu, "Fiscal Federalism and Provincial Foreign Tax Policies in China," *Journal of Contemporary China,* 15,48, (August, 2006): 479-502.

Zhu, Yuchao and Dongyan Blachford, "Ethnic Minority Issues in China's Foreign Policy: Perspectives and Implications, *The Pacific Review,* Vol. 18 No. 2 (June 2005): 243–264.

Zweig, David, *Internationalizing China: Domestic Interests and Global Linkages,* (Ithaca: Cornell University Press, 2002).

Index